SO YOU WANT TO BE A LEADER!

Kenneth O. Gangel

So You Want to Be a Leader!

Basic Principles and Methods of Christian Leadership

Christian Publications

Camp Hill, Pennsylvania

Christian Publications
3825 Hartzdale Drive, Camp Hill, PA 17011

The mark of ✝ vibrant faith

ISBN: 0-87509-421-X
LOC Catalog Card Number: 88–93032
© 1973, 1989 by Christian Publications
All rights reserved
Printed in the United States of America

94 93 92 91 90   8 7 6 5

To my students at

Calvary Bible College
Trinity Evangelical Divinity School
Miami Christian College
Dallas Theological Seminary

many of whom have already become
Christian leaders around the world.

CONTENTS

INTRODUCTION

A FEW YEARS AGO *Leadership Journal* ran a survey on lay leadership within the church. Response to that survey indicated that motivating and sustaining active participation of lay leaders is one of the most frustrating problems facing pastors today. Yet lay leadership is the genius of the New Testament church.

Many of the problems in lay leadership can be attributed to spiritual immaturity, but many also stem from a failure to grasp the basic components of a leadership role. This book is designed as a basic primer in addressing those problems. It distills the strategic ideas found in my two larger volumes on the subject—*Building Leaders for Church Education* (Moody) and *Feeding and Leading* (Victor).

Kenneth O. Gangel
Dallas, Texas

So You Want to Be a Leader!

JOHN HAS JUST BECOME the Sunday school superintendent at First Church. The church is not large by modern standards, approximately 170, but John suddenly realizes that he is about to pass from the ranks of the followers to the ranks of the leaders. This is not John's first ministry; he has held various positions (teacher of junior high boys and member of the Christian education committee), but these positions always found him dependent upon someone else for his decisions. Now, as an administrator with oversight of the Sunday school staff, John is responsible for getting things done through other people.

You may be like John. Perhaps you are not a Sunday school superintendent, but any position of supervisory oversight within a group requires awareness of leadership roles and responsibilities. Whom would that include? Parents, pastors, general superintendents, departmental superintendents, club program leaders, youth sponsors, committee chairmen, board members and all other Christian leaders whose relationships to people require them to direct the goals and activities of a group through the influence of their abilities, personalities and techniques.

What is Christian leadership? A more complete answer to that question must await the second chapter. In this initial chapter I propose to take a broad overview of some of the principles of personality and ability found in effective leaders—things you must learn in order to function effectively in a leadership position.

Responsibility

Simply defined, *responsibility* is the willingness to make decisions and stand by them. It recognizes that leadership requires an openness to "burden bearing" and task accomplishment. Local churches sometimes have difficulty in recruiting leaders, because people simply do not want the responsibility.

Why? Because the responsibilities of leadership are not always pleasant. Often they represent work that no one else is willing to do. So part of the price of leadership is the willingness to assume those tasks, perhaps even because no one else wants to do them.

Oral communication

Adolph Hitler once said, "The power that has set in motion the greatest avalanches in politics and religion has been, from the beginning of time, the magic of the spoken word." Whatever we may think of Hitler's political ideals, we will have to admit that he is right about the significance of the spoken word. For salesmen, the power of the spoken word involves primarily the motivational ability of persuading people to make decisions about a product. For Christians, it involves the communication of a biblical message.

Certainly not all effective leaders are good public speakers, but it is safe to say that those who can communicate will be better leaders because of it. Effective public speaking includes the ability to "think on one's feet" as well as skill in the delivery of a manuscript address. As the ancient Greeks emphasized in the days of Demosthenes, skill in speaking can be developed. One of the later chapters of this book will deal with just that subject.

Bible knowledge

Is the message more important than the method, or the method more important than the message? Some would be tempted to maintain that the message largely determines the method. In the final analysis, however, this false dichotomy leads to futile argument. Both a ship without a cargo or a cargo without a ship would be meaningless to people waiting on the opposite shore for delivery of much-needed goods.

Christian leaders cannot afford to be ignorant of the one message central to all their activities. They must not only be interested in Bible study and in reading the things others have learned, they must also become independent investigators of the Word of God. Remember Jehovah's command to Joshua: "Do not let this Book of the Law depart from your mouth; meditate on it day and night, so that you may be careful to do everything written in it. Then you will be prosperous and successful" (1:8).

Interest in and understanding of people

A biblical view of leadership will always find us exercising great concern for the needs and interests of our co-workers. Human relations in the church is not only a means to an end but an end in itself. Such a genuine concern for working effectively with people must include the development of the leader's own personality. It will probably lead him or her to participatory rather than autocratic leadership. Even secular views of leadership direct an increasing focus on the leader as a member of a group who leads that group toward its goals. A sensitivity to successful human relations will help leaders avoid the unpleasant traits of their own personality such as selfishness, faultfinding, sarcasm, defensiveness, self-pity, anger and moodiness. Such self-indulgence, frequently found in followers, the truly effective Christian leader cannot afford.

Neatness of dress and behavior

Scripture teaches that people look on the outward appearance, but God looks on the heart. If the only concern were for a relationship with God, the Christian leader probably would have less pressure at this point. But leadership, although based on a vertical relationship with God, finds implementation on the horizontal plane. Consequently, what people think about the way we look will have positive or negative effects on our leadership.

The leader should be clean and neatly dressed, demonstrating at the same time an awareness of contemporary styles and the moderation clearly called for in the New Testament. Demeanor and decorum should make this person pleasant to be with rather than one to be avoided because he or she is sloppy, loud or boorish.

Dependability

Some have considered this to be the cardinal virtue of leadership. Dependable people always come through on their word. They answer their correspondence within a reasonable time. They do not misplace notes or forget appointments. They do not allow names to slip their mind, embarrassing people or contributing to the ineffectiveness of the organization. They do not rationalize their difficulties in leadership or blame them on other people.

In contrast, they consistently turn in the kind of job expected of them by superiors and/or subordinates. Their dependability also implies a high degree of faithfulness and loyalty to the group.

Organizational ability

Leaders stand directly responsible for group goal achievement. Their work includes delegation, decision-making, planning and organization. Part of this involves developing other leaders, helping them to see the coherence of the organization's task. Another part is the communication of essential information. Still another part is the willingness to let group members make their own decisions, encouraging them to work together toward goal achievement. Understanding group goals and the relationship of people in an organization helps leaders know how to develop programs that are interesting, informative and need-meeting.

Willingness to work

Leadership often seems never ending. Usually the followers can "turn off" the demands of the organization when the day ends. But leaders just transfer the base of operations from one place to another and continue to carry out their responsibilities. There is no room here for the temperamental hero who wants nothing more from leadership than the adoring cheers of a worshipful crowd. His or her example in the nitty-gritty work of the organization will often be the inspiration necessary to motivate group members.

Courage and patience

Each element of the leadership role should be listed separately and thus carry its own emphasis. Yet this combination (courage and patience) seems to be justified because both have to do with the difficulties that we encounter as we try to bring about change and innovation in the organization. They are inextricably woven into the process of getting along with other people.

The old cliche "if you don't understand it, oppose it" often seems to be the norm in the church. The leader finds him or herself desperately in need of patience to wait for the process of change to take effect. Leaders—usually initiators of change in existing structures—must have courage to face sometimes hostile attitudes. As one pastor put it with tongue in cheek, "In my church, change is sin, and we sin as little as possible."

Popularity is rarely the most important result of leadership! The loneliness experienced by some leaders of the Old Testament (Moses, David, Elijah) offers a clear example of the reason why Jehovah told Joshua three times in the first nine verses of the first chapter that he must be courageous if he was to assume command of Israel at that crisis point in its history.

Creativity

Leadership can provide creative administration or it can degenerate into custodial management. The former brings the organization and its people to progressive ways and patterns without destroying the initial objectives and standards of earlier days. The latter emphasizes maintenance and "keeping the lid on" so that nothing that goes wrong will be attributed to the leader.

A creative person has the ability to bring into existence something unusual. It might be a teaching method; it might be a promotional idea; it might be a decoration for a party. It always comes out of the development of an imaginative mind—a mind sensitive to surroundings, open to ideas and new thought patterns and characterized by independent and reflective thinking.

In a real sense, the creative person is a dreamer dissatisfied with the way things are or have been, because he or she consistently thinks they could be better. The best research on the subject of creativity indicates that creative people are made not born; creativity is basically a capacity for the restructuring and reforming of ideas. It can be learned and taught.

All 10 of these ingredients that go into making an effective leader are attainable by most people reading this chapter. Each ingredient can be developed from study, practice and consistent learning. Although some seem rather mundane and earthbound when viewed in the context of Christian leadership, all depend upon the work of the Spirit, the will of God, the power of the Word and the significance of prayer.

Leadership means coordinating the energy and motivation of a group to accomplish its purposes. When we bring these qualities to the task, we just begin the difficult process of leadership. The chapters ahead will attempt to show how some of the more specific processes can be carried out to achieve genuinely spiritual, competent and dynamic Christian leadership.

2

Understanding Christian Leadership

O NE DAY WHILE TEACHING His disciples, Jesus expressed a principle of frightening dimensions: "Much is required from those to whom much is given, for their responsibility is greater" (Luke 12:48, LB). The context is the parable of the two servants. The faithful and wise servant described in verses 41–44 receives the appointment of leadership by rising from the ranks of the slaves. Like Joseph of old, he is sovereignly appointed by the lord of the household to a place of supervision over others. Because of his faithfulness as ruler over the household, he eventually becomes "ruler over all," a position of important leadership. In contrast is the faithless and foolish servant described in verses 45–48a. His motivation for behavior centers in the anticipation that he will not get caught. As soon as he concludes that "no one will see me," the inner nature comes out and he behaves in a shameful fashion. His retribution is to receive an appointment with the unbelievers to punishment and loss.

Two crucial principles can be drawn from this parable in Luke 12. The first has already been suggested above: leaders exercise a greater responsibility and will have to answer to Christ. The second principle teaches that both servants, in their initial positions of leadership as lords of the household, shared a responsibility to know the will of the master. The parable makes it plain that those who know God's will and do not do it and those who do not know God's will are punished *because both had responsiblity for knowing*. Notice, however, that the leader who knew the will of God and did not do it was punished to a greater extent. Although it has often been applied as an argument for salvation, this parable is hardly a story about evangelism. The context and language of the parable require a recognition of responsibilities in Christian service, and particularly in Christian leadership.

Defining a leadership style

Sometimes we think of leaders as possessing certain *characteristics* or *traits* that mark them as people who occupy a status position somewhat higher than their peers. Other times leaders represent the consequence of the needs of a group of people. Here the emphasis is on goal achievement and effectiveness of group guidance, whereas the former idea focuses on the leader as a symbol. One might be termed "mythical leadership" and the other "functional leadership." Both views look at the leader through the eyes of his or her group or of his or her followers.

Leadership style may also be defined in terms of *how the leader views his subordinates*. Here a threefold division seems better. Although we could use various terms for these three approaches to leadership, we will call them *autocratic, free-rein* and *participatory*.

Autocratic leaders are trait-centered. They view themselves in a steryotyped way. They feel that they alone can direct the activities of the group satisfactorily and that, because of their greater knowledge or ability, group members must give implicit obedience to their commands. Sometimes they "drive" the group toward their own ends rather than fulfilling collective needs they might sense in the group. This kind of leader is common in Christian circles, because we tend to confuse scriptural authority with our own.

The *free-rein leader* tends to be person-centered, focusing on group members. The group proceeds at its own rate, with a strong dependence on personal initiative and self-guidance. New forms of "discovery learning" represent this kind of nondirective leadership. Sometimes persons opt for this style for the wrong motives. If, for example, a leader exercises free-rein leadership because he or she really believes the group can proceed better on its own, then the choice is well made. If, on the other hand, the leader is merely shrinking from responsibility, then he or she may hinder the effectiveness of the group.

The *participatory leader* leads in a method that is approved by modern management specialists—and is also the style most favored in the New Testament. This median approach is primarily a guiding relationship. Group-oriented leaders provide general supervision, but they never look over shoulders to make sure people do things their way.

Participatory leaders share responsibilities of decision-making and planning with group members rather than superimposing their ideas. People tend to think of them as team members, leaders among equals.

The element of "situation" also enters into a definition of this kind of leadership. Certainly leadership traits are important; God does gift certain people to carry out His work. And the group is important, because responsibility sharing is a positive reflection of New Testament patterns. "Situation" suggests that leadership may be limited by certain contexts in which the leader performs. Andrew Halpin has summed it up well:

> In a specific situation, leaders do have traits that set them apart from the followers, but what traits set what leader apart from what followers will vary from situation to situation.[1]

All things considered, Christian leaders must recognize their own gifts, the needs and goals of their people and organization and the various situations in which they find themselves before identifying or selecting a leadership style. Most of us will probably choose a participatory approach. But there will be those rare situations in which we should be flexibile enough to slide toward free-rein or autocratic leadership when those styles are needed.

Developing your spiritual gifts

New Testament teaching on spiritual gifts is provided mainly in four passages: Romans 12:3–8; First Corinthians 12; Ephesians 4:11–16; and First Peter 4:10. The Greek word *charisma* used in each of these cases appears 17 times as a noun. Fifteen of those times, it is translated as "gift" and 2 times as "free gift." Interestingly enough, apart from the passage in First Peter 4:10, it is used only by Paul. The obvious distinction in these passages is the description of some unique capacity for ministry.

Having a spiritual gift does not imply that a person will automatically perform at a certain level. What would you think, for example, if your pastor indicated some day that he has the "gift of teaching," and therefore, it will never be necessary for him to do any more preparation? From now on he will stand in the pulpit twice on Sunday and say whatever comes into his head, because he is just "exercising his spiritual gift." Obviously, such glorification of ignorance is far from the New Testament intent.

From First Corinthians 12 we understand at least four basic principles regarding the possession and utilization of spiritual gifts.

1. *Spiritual gifts are given to everybody.* Surely some Christians have more than one spiritual gift, but no Christian can accurately say that he or she has *no* spiritual gifts. Paul states in First Corinthians 7:7 that "each man has his own gift from God; one has this gift, another has that." Paul reinforces this statement in the 12th chapter, verse 11: "All these are the work of one and the same Spirit, and he gives them to each man, just as he determines."

2. *Spiritual gifts are given in sovereignty.* Although it seems possible for the Christian to ask God for certain spiritual gifts (v. 31), no gift can be usurped or grasped apart from the will of God. Gifts make possible the healthy life of the church in the world. It suits God's purposes to offer them in accordance with His plans.

3. *Spiritual gifts are to be exercised in unity.* Paul belabors this issue throughout the central part of the 12th chapter. Using the analogy of the physical body, he emphasizes again and again how all parts of the body have their distinctive roles. Yet those roles are worthless apart from collective unity and community.

4. *Spiritual gifts are to be exercised in love.* Keeping in mind that chapter divisions do not come along with the inspired text, see how closely chapter 13 follows hard on the heels of chapter 12. To put it simply, exercise of a spiritual gift apart from love is worthless futility on the part of the Christian leader.

First Corinthians 12 and similar passages in the New Testament show that Christian leadership is really the exercise of spiritual gifts. But those gifts are capacities to be trained, so we need to consider such seemingly mundane matters as definitions of leadership, leadership style, relationships to other people and many more. The trick is to keep things in balance: the distinct biblical, spiritual callings and gifts on the one hand and the development and polishing of those capacities for leadership on the other.

Exercising Christian discipline

In a loose society full of permissive ideas, few people like to talk about discipline. Yet one clarion call rings throughout the pages of Scripture and the ages of history: great leaders, both Christian and non-Christian, have always been disciplined persons. They learned to prescribe boundaries for their own behavior.

Christian discipline can be of three types: enforced or external discipline, such as we must use for children and immature people; self-discipline, primarily comprised of adult attitudes and decisions; and Christ-discipline, which is based on Christian surrender. A Christ-disciplined leader becomes a Christ-controlled self. But Christian leaders must still take responsibility for personal discipline rather than always needing the encouragement and push of other people.

The word *discipline* relates closely to the word *discipleship*. Both connote living the controlled life. Just as a girl settles finally to the one man who becomes her husband, so the Christian leader settles into a ministry to which God has called him or her. At times such a decision pushes out other good things just as the selection of a husband pushes out other good men. Such a narrowing process, however, is a part of Christ self-discipline.

Discipline also helps us understand that we do not punch clocks on an eight-hour day. If leadership responsibility is full-time, our work may never be done. We need to program in time for family, time for refreshing recreational activities and time for rest. We will come back to this in chapter three.

Christian leaders who recognize that ultimate discipline comes from above and submit to it, stand in a position of discipleship. Actually, discipline may operate at three levels: (1) leaders receive discipline from Christ, the Head of the church; (2) leaders discipline themselves as they live controlled and balanced lives; and (3) leaders exercise discipline with others, helping them to become disciples. How can we make progress toward effective Christ self-discipline? Certainly no "one-a-day pills" will produce this kind of mature attitude. Nevertheless, some guidelines can help.

Begin now. It is never too early to regiment oneself into this kind of life. As a matter of fact, those of us who are parents ought to be nurturing our children toward disciplined living from their earliest days.

Pattern your life after God's Word. Remember Moses, whose disciplined life required him to exercise enormous self-restraint in listening for 40 years to the murmuring and complaining of Israel. Remember Joshua, who was able to say, even at the end of his lifetime of struggle, "As for me and my house, we will serve the Lord." Remember the Hebrew children in Babylon, who renounced all political advantages to say that they would not be defiled with the king's meat. Remember the apostle Paul, whose faithful missionary efforts took him again and again into hard places, whose spiritual struggles incarnated maturity and discipline.

Commit yourself to the control of the Holy Spirit. In Ephesians 5, God teaches us that being filled with the Spirit centers in His absolute control of our lives day by day. This is not some elaborate ritual, but a simple dependence upon and commitment to His working in us.

Set goals and strive for them. Be a dreamer. Think big; but always think within the will of God. When God gives the green light on a certain project, we should do it with all our ability and His power.

Above all, do not be a quitter. Like Jeremiah, let us feel the fire in our bones thrusting us so strongly into Christian leadership that we will be unable to quit! Perhaps the key verse in the New Testament with respect to this kind of living is Luke 9:23: "Then he said to all, 'Anyone who wants to follow me must put aside his own desires and conveniences and carry his cross with him every day and keep close to me!'" (LB).

Planning Your Life

WHAT ARE THE GOALS OF YOUR LIFE? Have you ever written them down? Meaningless expenditure of time tends toward purposelessness and kills motivation. One of the great themes of the Psalmist, which ought to be meaningful to us in this "pressure cooker" age, is that his times were in God's hands (31:15). If we believe that God sovereignly controls time, then insufficient time—a common complaint among leaders—is neither a problem nor an excuse for things left undone. *The weakness lies in planning and investment of our time.*

Many of us find ourselves in the position of constant reaction. Rather than controlling the events of a given day (as much as possible), we tend to be constantly governed by the events themselves. To put it another way, rather than managing our work, we allow our work to manage us. We exercise our leadership like a small boy with a large dog on a leash. Without traditions and patterns to which our families and organizations have been accustomed through the years, our lives would be even more shaky than they are now.

The secret of successful leadership is to live and move *above* the circumstances and thereby exercise as much control upon them as possible. This does not in any way usurp the authority of God as sovereign Controller of all circumstances. Rather we try to find His will, then act objectively toward the fulfillment of that will by planning a constant pattern of goal achievement.

Time is a commodity to be invested. For years we Americans have raped our natural resources. The ecology movement arose to call our attention to the fact that there will not always be water, trees, mountains and other natural resources. Time is being dissipated at a much more rapid and consistent rate than even natural resources.

Some years ago a tape on which I had dictated an entire chapter for a new book was accidentally erased. Apart from the scattered notes and outlines from which I worked, there was no way to recall what was gone. One day of my life had been lost, and there was no way to reclaim it; I would never see it again.

Establishing priorities

All Christians (and certainly all Christian leaders) should have a written list of life goals that they feel are within the will of God for them to accomplish during the 60 or 70 years they may expect to live on the earth. This is not a project that can be done in 15 minutes. It requires a significant investment of time to achieve a satisfactory product.

Not only that, but the juggling of priorities within that listing of life goals may be a constant process. In other words, a current primary goal might change in two or three years as God gives further information and direction with respect to one's life. Changing the plan from time to time is not wrong. Failure comes from not having a plan at all!

One of the most effective books on managing one's life and work wisely is J.W. Alexander's *Managing Our Work*, published by Inter-Varsity Press. In that volume the author offers a model that suggests setting overall objectives into more specific goal implementations, which are governed, in turn, by standards of behavior.[2]

The following chart, adapted from Alexander's model, will no doubt seem traditional to the prophets of change. It is, however, based upon the premise that the local church is a New Testament insitution and will exist in some form until the return of our Lord.

Purpose: To serve Christ with my life and my time.
Objective: To be a faithful and active member of a local church.
Goal: 1 – To be regular in attendance at services of my church.
Realization Procedures:
a. I actively seek fellowship and worship experiences with other believers.

b. I seek to be of assistance to other members of the body in any way I can.

c. I make an effort to exercise practical love in my relationships with other believers in the local church.

Goal: 2 – To support my church in every way possible.
Realization Procedures:
a. I give proportionately of my income so that the work of the church can be maintained and furthered.

b. I encourage my children, my friends and my neighbors to recognize and carry out the biblical imperatives with respect to the local church.

c. I recognize my part in the planning and progress that my church must carry on to exercise its proper ministry in the community.

Goal: 3 – To effectively share in the work of the church.

Realization Procedures:

a. I recognize my spiritual gifts and attempt to utilize them within the framework of the church.

b. I encourage others to recognize and use their spiritual gifts within the framework of the church.

c. I depend upon the power of the Holy Spirit to enable me to teach or minister in whatever way God has led me to do so within the structure of the church.

There is ample room within the statements above for structural change and flexibility. There is no room, however, for an attitude that relegates all structure and form to the junk heap of anachronism. In actually developing life objectives, goals and standards, you will multiply the above model several times as you delineate the things God has specifically planned for you.

Be realistic in listing your life goals. Avoid spiritualizing. If you intend to become president of your company, then list that. Write all these things and then take a good look at the priority listings that you have chosen. It only makes sense to invest your time in proportion to your priorities. If the really important thing in your life is to become president of your company, then it may be necessary to bypass a lot of other things that clamor for attention but are of lesser importance.

Paying attention to levels of planning

Once priorities are clearly defined, you can implement your goals and live by your standards. As you begin planning, think on at least five levels.

Level 1: The plan for my total life. Decisions both large and small enter into this plan. For example, if your life plan is to become a college professor, that obviously will include some major time investment in formal schooling and the earning of degrees. If your plan includes the winning of a salesmanship award with your company, then the development of your sales techniques and knowledge of products and territories will earn priority rating. If you plan to be an independent student of the Bible, then you know you must invest time in inductive Bible study and probably in building a personal library of helpful volumes.

Level 2: The plan for a year. Keep in mind that I am still talking about planning your personal life and not the program of the church. In the same way that you record long-range objectives for the ministry of your life, you can record objectives for a given year. This involves spelling out certain tasks, both large and small, that you want to see accomplished in your life and/or home during any given year.

Level 3: The plan for a month. In a real sense, the plan for a month is just one of 12 steps toward the total plan for a year. Since different kinds of things happen at different seasons of the year, the monthly plans will not all be alike. They will, however, be carefully coordinated so that when put together, they form a more specific yearly plan.

Level 4: The plan for a week. Weeks go by so rapidly. You have to determine at the beginning of the week what steps must be taken toward goal achievement over the seven-day period. Do not forget to program in times for rest, recreation and family fun as well as the nitty-gritty aspects of the work plan.

Level 5: The plan for a day. Plans for years and months are important, but life unfolds one day at a time. Scripture is intensely practical when it says "Each day has enough trouble of its own" (Matthew 6:34b). Jim Spillman, former administrative pastor at Calvary Temple in Denver, suggests an interesting seven-step technique for carrying out a daily plan. Its components include:

    a. the day-before carryover
    b. the early-morning reflection
    c. the immediate attack
    d. the midday review
    e. the five o'clock review
    f. the before-bed evaluation
    g. the final action – culmination or projection

Of course, to be practical, this must be done in writing in order to have constantly before you the unfolding task of the day. Keep an accurate calendar, by the telephone or in your pocket, that provides ready access for appointments or other responsibilites throughout the day.

Building a life pattern

Another factor that relates to organizing our personal lives through careful planning is the matter of motivation. Here I do not mean the motivation of other people, but personal motivation – those stimulating forces that cause us to select priorities and deliberately move objectively toward goal realization.

One way of looking at such forces is to think of them as component parts of a value system. For example, a man who truly values his role as father and head of the family will construct his life pattern so that a significant portion of his time can be spent with that family. A woman who sets a life goal of breaking all the sales records of her company will find great reinforcement in each award that comes her way and will be motivated toward greater heights of salesmanship every time a customer signs a new contract.

Sometimes the factors of motivation are not quite so external and obvious. The ministry of a pastor, for example, may pass through many months before he sees his work reinforced by definite spiritual growth in the lives of the people in his congregation. To see it, however, is to experience a continuing motivation that thrusts him back to prepare even more provocative and edifying messages that will in turn produce the same kind of personal growth in other people.

Perhaps the most significant kind of motivation is a calm assurance that we do what we do because of God's call. In those parched periods when no visible results can be found to reinforce our efforts, that recognition can provide the necessary fuel to keep the fires of leadership burning.

CHAPTER

4

Organizing Your Work

P EOPLE WHO HAVE LEARNED TO MANAGE their own lives can play a key part in transferring that organized life-style to their work within the church or other organizations. Just as they have established their own well-defined goals, they take the broader view and assist the organization in clarifying its goals and in moving objectively toward goal realization.

In two other books on the subject of leadership, I have devoted several pages to principles of organization.[3] Without reproducing them here, let me just say that an understanding of these basic principles is fundamental to proper functioning in the church. In addition, only properly functioning organizational patterns can give birth to clear goals.

Clarifying your goals

I recently read an interesting article on clarifying goals. The opening paragraph summed up its thrust:

> Of all corporate attitudes, the most important is orientation toward objectives. That's the management attitude that creates an environment in which objectives are enunciated, developed and attained—or not attained. Every decision you or your company makes, big or small, is influenced by orientation. Perhaps it's time to take a good hard look at it.[4]

The article goes on to suggest that we analyze our work to determine whether we are problem-oriented or objective-oriented in articulating our goals and gives four steps to help us come up with the answer.

1. *Take a good, hard look at the competition.* An objective-oriented company will have a good record of new ideas when compared with other organizations doing the same thing. Could not local churches implement this same kind of examination with respect to other churches of the same basic size and denomination in the same area of the country?

2. *Look back over changes that have taken place in your industry in the past three years.* If they have come about because of pressure from the competition, then your institution is probably problem-oriented. If, on the other hand, changes have come because there is an innovative and progressive mind-set in the organization, then you may be exercising management by objectives.

3. *Appraise the out-of-step leader.* If the organization is problem-oriented, then the objective-oriented leader will be the one who appears to be thinking differently from everyone else in the organization. It could be that "personality clashes" arise primarily from orientation.

4. *Examine conversations for symptoms of problem-orientation.* Consider the last church business meeting or meeting of the Christian education board or committee. How much time did you spend discussing objectives and goal achievement and how much time discussing problems? Problems will come, but the objective-oriented institution *controls* its problems rather than *being controlled* by them.[5]

Changing problem-oriented objectives

If after such self-examination you decide that your

church or organization is problem-oriented, these steps may help to lead in a different direction:

1. *Organize the decision-making process for objective orientation.* In the objective-oriented institution, ideas and innovations cannot be dismissed simply by saying, "We don't have the money." Not having the money stands as a roadblock to goal achievement. Consequently, it becomes our task not to stop there but to discover how that barrier can be removed so that the goal can be achieved. Rather than "We don't have the money," our concern then becomes, "What are several realistic ways we can get the money?"

2. *Eliminate timidity.* In describing this step, the article identifies the desirable orientation:

> A proper management climate is one [that] shares honest mistakes with the people making them; [that] considers inaction as the greatest sin; [that] gives plenty of room to its people to innovate on their own and encourages problem-solving skills and objective-oriented people.[6]

3. *Delegate!* Leaders should supervise the maximum number of people they can effectively manage. Within that span of control, they delegate everything that they cannot do themselves. Right? Wrong! Within that span of control they *only do themselves what they cannot delegate!* Of course, in the process of delegation they recognize that the leader is always accountable for the actions of the subordinates and that whenever possible, people should be accountable to only one superior.

Unless a Sunday school is small (3–9 teachers), the superintendent cannot supervise the whole team. Instead he or she concentrates attention on the direction and coordination of departmental superintendents. He or she delegates to them a large part of the responsibilities and authority for the ongoing activities in their particular departments.

By the same token, the teachers in those departments are accountable *not* to the general superintendent but to the departmental superintendent. Requests for supplies, complaints about facilities and ideas for innovations are given to their departmental superintendents who, in turn, direct them to the general superintendent. When appropriate, he or she shares them with the board of Christian education.

4. *Eliminate long lead times between setting objectives and targeting completion dates.* Objective-oriented leadership works best when most of our objectives can be achieved within a reasonable time frame.

That achievement should be visible, and in order to be reinforcing, it has to provide positive experiences for the people in the organization. Like children, adults have a limited attention span and can keep their energies focused on a given objective or set of objectives for only a limited amount of time. Enthusiasm can die on the vine if it is not rewarded by periodic goal achievement. Growth is achieved by piling one attained objective on top of another.

Charting project organization

One other phase of organization, which might bear mentioning in this chapter, is what professional management calls *project organization*. It deals with the handling of a given project or event rather than with the care of the ongoing organization from month to month and year to year. Much church work comes at us like a string of projects stretched end to end.

Throughout any given year, for example, a senior high

youth group may be involved in 10 or 12 different projects covering such areas as visitation, fund-raising for a certain goal, work projects (painting a part of the church building), service projects (singing and witnessing at a rest home once a month), training projects (youth retreat) or missionary projects (spending two weeks on an Indian reservation in Colorado or Arizona). As the youth sponsor and the teen leaders administer the activities of a group like this, they are engaged in constant project management.

Project organizing requires that clear culmination of the project be in sight. It has finite time limits, almost always less than a year in duration. There are some notable exceptions, though, such as a church committee that may be planning a centennial celebration by working on the project for two or three years before it actually occurs.

For the sake of illustration, assume that you are the chairperson of the Christian education committee and it is your task to plan an annual three-day leadership-training retreat. Handling this event for any year is project organization. What steps do you follow in carrying it out?

• Develop the general requirements and characteristics of the project, establishing the overall objectives.

• Prepare the specifications for the retreat that would involve such essential factors as time, place and financing.

• Establish what is called the "support-ability" for the plans already made. In other words, can you actually carry out the tentative requirements that you have designated for the project?

• Establish equipment resources for whatever items are going to be needed. Do you have overnight accommodations? How will meals be planned and prepared? What kinds of "classroom" facilities do you need for the training?

• Develop a schedule for the weekend, coordinating it with the master schedule of the entire church calendar.

• Provide motivating publicity in order to get the most workers to attend the retreat.

• Identify on-location leadership. Will you conduct the training sessions yourself? What role will the pastor and/or the director of Christian education play? Will you be bringing in speakers from the outside?

• Develop the "operational logistics" that lead to satisfactory fulfillment of your objectives. Should there be preparation on the part of your people before they go to the retreat site? How will you coordinate the training sessions with the needs and objectives in the total educational program?

• Finally, evaluate. After the retreat, it is essential to analyze the results. What was the attendance level and why? What kind of feedback did people give you regarding their experiences? What strengths and weaknesses should you build in or avoid when planning the retreat for next year?

God is a God of order. The astronauts who walked on the moon testify to the meticulous consistency of the makeup of the universe. The regularity of the seasons establishes the norm and the pattern characteristic of the Creator. In that same pattern, Christian leaders must organize the activities of their own work so that they reflect the careful order demonstrated by God.

CHAPTER
5

Knowing Where You're Going (And How to Get There)

ONCE YOU HAVE BEEN ABLE to successfully plan your own life and exercise self-discipline toward the achievement of personal objectives, then you are ready to be of service to your organization as a planner. Planning is one of the most strategic aspects of administration, and to some extent it is a part of the task of every leader. Many large corporations employ entire staffs or departments to do nothing but work on planning. They assume that if the organization is to achieve its goals, retain and expand its part of the market, they must aim its activities in the direction of accomplishing its goals. Abraham Lincoln said, "If we could first know where we are, and whither we are tending, we could better judge what to do and how to do it."

One basic implication of planning, whether it be for General Motors or for a growing Sunday school of 100, is the pronounced cause-effect relationship between events. The modern systems approach to administration helps us recognize that spiritual or numerical growth in a local church relates to size, organization, finances, facilities, instructional quality and a number of other concrete and visible factors as well as to the spiritual (invisible) factors readily acknowledged. Because planning fits into all these areas, it provides a common denominator to all parts of the system.

Forty years ago administration was conceived of as a neat package of planning, organizing, staffing, directing, coordinating, reporting and budgeting or some similar listing of managerial tasks. But this eight-step procedure (developed by Luther Gulick and given the acronym POSDCORB) is much too simple to describe the leadership demands of contemporary society.

Today most churches and Christian organizations see the need for systematic planning. They recognize that the findings of managerial research can be easily adapted to the church's situation, providing help in achieving our biblical objectives. The key to the whole process is the leader. That person may not always be the one responsible for the planning, but he or she must make sure that planning takes place and that the plans are implemented in the daily functioning of the organization.

What is long-range planning?

Louis A. Allen in *The Management Profession* defined *planning* as "the work a manager performs to predetermine a course of action."[7] He includes seven basic steps or aspects to the planning process:

Forecasting: the work a manager performs to estimate the future.
Establishing Objectives: the work a manager performs to determine the end results to be accomplished.
Programming: the work a manager performs to establish the sequence and priority of action steps to be followed in reaching objectives.
Scheduling: the work a manager performs to establish a time sequence for programmed steps.

Budgeting: the work a manager performs to allocate
resources necessary to accomplish objectives.

Establishing Procedures: the work a manager performs
to develop and apply standardized methods of per-
forming specified work.

Developing Policies: the work a manager performs to
develop and interpret standing decisions that apply to
repetitive questions and problems of significance to
the enterprise as a whole.[8]

In its simplest form planning attempts to identify trends
and then devise a program to fit into those trends in order
to continue accomplishing the objectives. Planning almost
always proceeds on a basis of past experience and present
information.

We could say that planning attempts to somehow identify the winds of change in order to more properly set our
sails. Not that the winds themselves determine the direction of the organizational vessel, but rather that, knowing
the direction of the wind and the tide, the leader can
more correctly steer the vessel to the intended port.

The process of planning is inseparably related to the
objectives of the organization. Assume that you are the
planning leader for a church of 250 members. In order to
make any headway in long-range planning, the objectives
of that church must be spelled out to cover all aspects of
its programming and to describe that program with a high
degree of specificity. Being specific about objectives means
more than just commitment to worship, fellowship, in-
struction and evangelism. Each of these categories of
church life must raise important issues for decisions that
are taken into consideration in planning. In short, the
organization that has fuzzy objectives will also have inadequate or inaccurate planning.

A biblical planning model

Planning is neither unspiritual nor unscriptural. As a matter of fact, Scripture gives us many examples of long-range planning. One of the best demonstrations in the New Testament is the care exercised by the apostle Paul in establishing converts, providing leadership and doing all that he could to ensure that the churches he started on his various missionary journeys would continue.

But the best biblical model of planning comes from the pages of the first book of the Old Testament. In Genesis 41, Joseph has just interpreted Pharaoh's dream. In effect, the dream projects the basic economic conditions for the land of Egypt for the next 14 years. Assuming reliable information about future phenomena, Joseph suggests a procedure for handling the situation:

> My suggestion is that you find the wisest man in Egypt and put him in charge of administering a nationwide farm program. Let Pharaoh divide Egypt into five administrative districts, and let the officials of these districts gather into the royal storehouses all the excess crops of the next seven years, so that there will be enough to eat when the seven years of famine come. Otherwise, disaster will surely strike (vv. 33–36, LB).

Joseph had never been to Harvard Business School. He had never attended an administration class, nor had he formally learned how to make a long-range plan. But he exhibits a gift from Jehovah that enables him to function as a competent administrator accomplishing God's purpose in Egypt at this point in history. To be sure, the whole situation of the famine is incidental to the real issue of the preservation and development of the nation of Israel. Nevertheless, we should look closely at the principles of leadership and administration we find tucked away within the accounts that comprise the history of God's people.

Perhaps it may help to recognize that Joseph's planning responsibility was unusual not only for him, but also for Egypt. Most of the Middle East depends upon rainfall for its crops; if there is a bad year, the food supply will be narrow. Egypt, however, depends upon the flooding of the Nile, a factor determined by the rains and snow in Africa and Abyssinia. A famine seldom occurred in the land of Egypt (a country called the "Grainary of Rome" at the time of Christ). So Joseph's responsibilities were not related to past experience. All planning had to proceed upon the basis of knowledge about present and future resources. The clear objective was to keep an entire nation alive while at the same time retaining absolute control for Pharaoh. Carefully read Genesis 41–47 to see how Joseph carried out his plan.

Measuring your planning responsibility

How much time does each person in the organization give to planning and how far in advance is that time invested? Planning time can be linked to thinking time and estimated percentages that various leaders in the organization should be devoting to thinking about long-range planning. I will translate the officers of industry (president, vice president, superintendent) into the officers of the church (pastor, director of Christian education, Sunday school superintendent) to show some representative figures. You can calculate the kind of input you are responsible for with respect to long-range planning.

By the standards of business and industry, the chief executive officer (pastor) should give less than 10 percent of his planning time to the immediate present, 10 percent to activities a month ahead and 10 percent to events that may be projected beyond five years. *His highest percentage of planning time aims at projections three to five years in the future,* at which point the American Management Association suggests a 30 percent investment of planning thought!

The director of Christian education invests 10 percent for one month ahead while only 20 percent is projected as far as three or four years. The Sunday school superintendent should be investing at least 20 percent of his or her planning time for next week but is down to 5 percent in the three- to four-year projection. Their highest investment of planning thought falls in the three- to six-month bracket. Classroom teachers, on the other hand, should be investing 40 percent of their planning time for next Sunday and only 2 percent for one year ahead. Few teachers hold any responsibilities for two years or beyond.

Variations in the figures do not change the obvious axiom: the higher the level of leadership in the organization, the greater the responsibility for long-range planning and the lesser the time given to thinking about immediate decisions and events close at hand.

Planning toward objectives

During the last two decades, management by objectives has become one of the most popular concepts in administrative procedure. Unfortunately, this all-purpose term means whatever a particular user chooses to define by it. The best approach to management by objectives looks at administration as a whole rather than at specific procedures for handling certain projects. The principle is simple: *progress can be measured only in terms of the ends toward which that progress is directed.*

Management by objectives can mean basically the same

thing in the church as it means in business and industry. The church that has adequately planned toward its objectives has emphasized specific goals to be established for each position and agency in the church. These goals identify the specific results to be achieved over a given period of time, usually a year. At the end of this period, *actual results achieved are measured against the original objectives planned and the results expected.* The point is that the leader should be measured by what he or she accomplishes in relation to what should be accomplished.

We can focus on mutual planning and problem solving rather than on an isolated worker's production performance as judged by his or her supervisor. A Christian education committee, for example, can properly evaluate teachers and workers only if they have adequate objectives and standards for every job, objectives that are understood by the committee and by the workers. The amount and direction of individual growth and improvement in job performance are then seen to be controlled largely by the quality of the objectives originally agreed upon.

Most churches cannot handle management by objectives simply because they do not have written statements that delineate their goals. They also fail to make it clear that *results are expected* for every service position in the church.

Remember, too, that objectives should be determined through communication and planning that flows in both directions. If your church has nothing in writing describing the role of Sunday school superintendent, the pastor and the director of Christian education should sit down with the superintendent to devise a mutually agreed upon standard of performance for his or her ministry. Of course, this would not have to be done every time a new superintendent comes to a task, but the personal interview *ex-*

plaining written standards is essential every time a new worker assumes a post.

Principles of long-range planning

Space will allow a descriptive listing of only 10 basic guidelines that will help to facilitate the planning process in an organization. Consider each one of them carefully and try to discover which ones you violate in your present leadership scheme.

1. *Planning is an investment, not an expenditure of time.* The farmer is not loafing while sharpening tools. Sometimes it appears we cannot afford the time to plan because of the pressure of daily activities. Of course, just the opposite is true; we cannot afford *not* to plan.

2. *Planning requires careful attention to immediate choices.* Immediate choices determine future choices. Think about the moon-shot programs for a moment. The module landed on the moon's surface because many decisions in the months preceding the landing aimed toward that ultimate goal. Any one of several decisions along the way could have negated the possibility of a lunar landing.

3. *Planning is cyclically based on evaluation.* In other words, we plan, carry out our plan and then evaluate the results. On the basis of the evaluation, we plan again, and the process starts all over.

4. *Planning requires acting objectively toward goal realization.* We must avoid what I called in one of my other books "drawing-board-itis"—the ability to construct ideas and plans in the solitude of an office, accompanied by a basic fear of getting them out into operation.

5. *Planning almost always leads to change.* Because change seems a basic threat to most people, carrying out a plan carries a number of roadblocks and pitfalls.

6. *Planning recognizes that an event will occur in ratio to*

its planning. Do you need a new building for the church? That building will become a reality only insofar as you plan effectively to build it.

7. *Planning increases in specificity as the event draws near.* We should be thinking today about the things we will do 10 years from now. Projecting that far in advance, however, enables us to consider only the most general ideas of what will happen then. As that planning point draws nearer, more specific plans must be delineated to meet it.

8. *Planning allows for maximum participation.* Most good plans include a lot of people. If we want people to work effectively in implementation, they should be included as much as possible in the planning stage. People will work more enthusiastically on a project if they have had a part in its planning.

9. *Planning requires an apportioning of thinking time.* We have already talked about this and established what I have called an axiom of administrative planning. Determine how much thinking time you should be giving to the future and how much you can afford to be spending on "here-and-now" activities.

10. *Planning recognizes that the effort applied should be commensurate with the results desired.* If the football team is going to win consistently, it will have to muster the necessary drive and determination to march off the field as victors each time they engage an opponent. If they only halfheartedly enter the ball game, they must expect to reap halfhearted results.

A difficult and complex task, planning requires special and deliberate effort. In reality, it could be said that we never really construct a "plan," because planning is a *process* that is always evolving. Even the term *construct* is dangerous—it might lead us to stop thinking about change and how we can adapt to a changing situation.

In his helpful book, *Tough-Minded Management*, J.D. Batten reminds us that

> A searching examination of the writings of the great philosophers reveals that growth, strength, and progress are closely dependent on planning, vision, and identification with the future. It is part of nature's plan that productivity and a sense of happiness are to a great extent related to a series of anticipation and a quickened interest in tomorrow.[9]

Like most aspects of leadership, planning is learned behavior. There are no "born planners." Let God develop in you those capacities and skills that can help your church look to the future with foresight and vision.

CHAPTER
6

Good Leaders Know
How to Think!

A GAME OF TIC-TAC-TOE SEEMS like a childishly simple exercise. Yet in the theoretical five moves, this game can be played 15,120 different ways. If this simple game has so many possibilities, how much more difficult is life? And how much more should go into the exercise of leadership, particularly the process of thinking and decision-making?

The author of the now famous book *The One Minute Manager* emphasizes that leadership is situational, governed by changing needs within the organization. Consequently, the way we make decisions relates precisely to how much or how little we involve people in those decisions and how much "managing" those people need. Here is how the author, Ken Blanchard, puts it.

> Americans must stop thinking in terms of extremes in leadership styles. Instead of gravitating to the extreme, managers should adopt the one best style of leadership that suits the people they supervise. Sometimes people need direction, and lots of it. Sometimes they need support and direction. And perhaps sometimes they just need to be left alone.[10]

Everyone agrees about the importance of thinking, but

not many people consider how it can be done effectively. We tend to accept the human mind as a functioning agent that will always be with us and can always be depended upon to do its task. The science of cybernetics has taught us a great deal about how the mind functions by studying the mechanical reproductions of that mind in the form of computers.

Putting your mind to work

When thinking about leadership, we must come eventually to problem-solving and decision-making. A "problem-oriented" leader (see chapter 4) tends to view the thinking task as difficult and "not much fun." He or she shies away from the apparent difficulties inherent in the working process of the human mind.

Every problem presents certain alternatives. When we sort out these alternatives, it becomes necessary to identify the better possible solutions. Then we follow through by evaluating the feasibility of these solutions. Failure to tolerate deferred judgment forces us to decide upon one of two or more courses of action too quickly. This can have disastrous results for our leadership.

Jean Buridan, a 14th century philosopher, spoke often of a certain donkey with a high IQ but a low capacity for making decisions. When placed midway between two equally attractive bundles of hay, it died of starvation because it could not find a valid reason to choose one or the other.

The opposite extreme attempts to make one over-simplified solution fit every problem. Then we become more like the medieval innkeeper who had only one bed. When a guest was too short for the bed, the innkeeper merely stretched his legs. If the guest was too tall, he accommodated the situation by chopping off enough of his legs to make him fit.

The process of thinking requires that crucial character-istic of purpose leading to the practical exploration of problem-solving solutions. We can direct our thinking negatively or positively. Dr. Norman Vincent Peale gained popularity with his book *The Power of Positive Thinking*. Its emphasis was on objective-oriented leadership.

In developing thought processes and deciding upon the amount of time and effort to put into thinking, we might do well to follow the pattern of the philosopher Rene Descartes. In *Discourse on Method* he delineates four prin-ciples that may be applied to the process of thinking and problem-solving.[11]

1. **The Principle of Evidence:** *Never accept as true anything we do not clearly know to be such.* This, again, involves the difficult process of deferred judgment. How foolish to think that the leader will ever have the opportu-nity to make a decision on the basis of "all the facts." In the first place, he or she will probably never learn "all the facts." In the second place, how are those "facts" to be interpreted? Or to put it another way, whose "facts" do we believe? Surely the law of evidence means that whereas we restrain ourselves from decision-making as long as we can to give ourselves the opportunity for as much information gathering as possible, in the final analysis there is still a highly subjective element in the decision itself. Indeed, in Christian leadership, the violation of Descartes's first prin-ciple is in a real sense the positive exercise of faith!

2. **The Principle of Analysis:** *Divide up problems and difficulties into as many parts as possible.* It is the analysis stage of the problem-solving process that seems to offer the most work for the least benefit. But that is not true. As a matter of fact, this "sorting process" of which Descartes

speaks is the heart of problem-solving. First we try to determine the real problem, and then we try to find the best possible solutions. Dividing the data into small chunks enables us to look at it more closely without being confused by the overly subjective nature of large blocks of information.

3. **The Principle of Method:** *We must conduct our thoughts in order, beginning with the simplest and easiest to know and proceeding in stages to the most complex knowledge.* Step two is analysis; step three is synthesis. It combines elements that are known to construct a whole.

Consider, for example, the work of a trial attorney as he prepares his client's case. He begins with the most obvious information, such as the generalized facts provided by the prosecution. As his investigation continues, however, he unearths linkage ideas and data that at first glance may seem irrelevant to the case. In the final analysis and in proper perspective, this data may actually provide the most significant component of the defense. The process of method should also cause us to get "ideas" about "facts." As we "hitchhike" on our own thoughts or on those of other people, we tend to build a construct of ideas that leads us to satisfactory solutions to the problems.

4. **The Principle of Control:** *Make surveys so wide and reviews so thorough and lists so complete as to be sure that nothing has been omitted.* Of course, Descartes was a hopeless idealist. I have already suggested that we can never depend on having all the facts. If we wait, as Descartes suggests, "to be sure that nothing has been omitted," then we shall still be waiting long after the time for final decision-making is past. With this kind of procrastination, we would soon find ourselves without leadership roles and therefore have no need to read this book. Nevertheless, the general intent of Descartes's remark is valid. He wants

us to cover our tracks. Without care for the process, an inferior or inadequate product may emerge. We dare not ignore some parcel or piece of information that ought to be plugged into the decision-making process.

Failure to reach for as much data as we can possibly grasp also leads to an extinguishing of the thought process at a premature hour. The story is often told of Hero of Alexandria, a mathematician and inventor who reportedly used steam in 100 B.C. to operate a toy. We can shrug off his experience as "an idea before its time," but what might have happened if Hero had asked some crucial questions about the process of his explorations? Can steam be of any use in anything but this toy? How could I possibly propel myself by means of this power? Is there any way that this force could be produced on a larger scale? Necessity may well be the mother of invention, but somewhere in the gestation period, the process of data gathering and deferred judgment makes a natural birth possible. And do not forget the midwife of objective decision-making.

The leader's thought processes must be inseparably connected with personal and/or organizational objectives. When compared with achievement of objectives, the saving of time seems an insignificant factor. The lesson is easily observed in the story of a fictitious airline pilot who made this announcement over the intercom:

Ladies and gentlemen, this is your captain speaking. We are presently flying at 25,000 feet through a very thick cloud cover somewhere over north central Colorado. There will be some choppiness because of the air currents, so we request that you keep your seat belts fastened. Just relax; there is nothing to worry about. We are hopelessly lost, but we are making good time!

The role of personality in decision-making

Man has gone to the computer for much of the decision-making process in education, business and industry because the computer can operate with data without corrupting it. Research in decision-making has shown that leaders will consistently undervalue the probabilities inherent in a problem-solving situation. This happens primarily because of a human conservatism toward risk.

Sometimes we make decisions on the basis of our feelings. We then have a tendency to follow up those decisions with rationalization in an attempt to convince ourselves (and perhaps others) that the decisions were right. Every time we think this way we make it a little easier to continue such irrational behavior and a little more difficult to retrace our steps. We must admit the emotional nature of our thought process, and begin recognizing the psychological factors involved in thinking and decision-making.

Thinking and decision-making *can* be improved, and the first step toward solving the problems of personality is to recognize that those problems exist and to take them into consideration in the problem-solving process. Howard K. Holland, writing in *Personnel Management,* suggests four steps that leaders should follow in coping with the personal elements of decision-making.[12]

1. *Know your own personality dynamics.* Are you primarily an optimistic person or a pessimistic person? Will your thinking be open-minded or will it tend to be limited and narrow? Do you have the patience to cope with deferred judgment, or do you feel that you must rush in to solve a problem with whatever information may be at hand? It does not take a professional analyst to help you take stock of yourself to see what kinds of attitudes may be coloring

your thinking process and thereby your personal and professional decisions.

2. *Set worthy goal pictures of yourself.* This is just a long-range production of the power of positive thinking. In other words, if you are an inadequate decision-maker right now, project a pattern and an image of how you will correct those problems and be a better decision-maker one, two or even five years from now. In setting realistic objectives and moving toward their achievement, you exercise the most rational part of your personality.

3. *Face reality objectively.* Try to shed the hiding mechanisms that corrupt your thinking process. Stop to analyze why you feel helpless or frustrated about a given situation. Why is it that you do not want to discuss a certain problem with your wife or husband? Is it clearly rational behavior to act this way? Why do you feel threatened when the assistant Sunday school superintendent comes into your office with some new idea? Are you perhaps an insecure person?

4. *Use your rational self deliberately.* Leaders *can* take over the direction of their lives. (Think back to some of the concepts of discipline discussed in chapter 2.) You can go about this by deliberately maintaining a balanced disposition that allows free operation of the power of the mind on the highest level.

St. Augustine attempted to come to grips with the negative elements of his personality by engaging in what he called "soliloquy." He would pit his Christian faith against secular reason in carrying out a series of questions and answers regarding God and his human soul. In short, he would *talk to himself.* It was not a monologue, but rather a debate geared to arrive at a satisfactory solution after honestly recognizing many of the elements that would tend to corrupt that solution.

Vertical versus lateral thinking

Edward de Bono, in the International Business Machines Corporation magazine *Think*, talks about "the virtues of zigzag thinking."[13] He decrys the fact that too much of our technique in decision-making falls into the vertical pattern. That is, we move in a stepwise process toward a certain goal. The information must be correct at every step, and we select and deal with only the relevant information. Such is the traditional pattern of decision-making.

Vertical thinking is then contrasted with *lateral thinking.* Lateral thinking is characterized by being nonsequential — it does not move logically step by step toward the goal. It does not have to be correct at every stage but can allow for a great deal of chaff to come in with the wheat, and it is not restricted to relevant information. This open-ended approach may lead us to conclusions not visible when we follow the traditional vertical process.

"In vertical thinking," says de Bono, "information is used for its own sake, as a contribution to the development of a structure. In lateral thinking, information is used provocatively in order to bring about a restructuring."[14] Lateral thinking rests on the premise that the mind is not just a machine that processes information. Rather, it is a total memory environment, which allows information to organize itself into categories.

Lateral thinking resembles brainstorming, but brainstorming is a particular technique. Lateral thinking is an attitude, an inventive approach to decision-making and problem-solving. It also varies from creativity, which emphasizes results and tends to make judgments on the basis of a finished product. Lateral thinking is a deliberate *process*, whether or not satisfactory results follow.

Think creatively

Creative thinking suffers from the widespread belief that it is something inherent in an individual and can never be learned. Recent research, however, denies that conclusion. *Creativity can be learned.* Learning to think creatively means producing some recombination of ideas or concepts by joining new behavior to old habits. Robert Fulton, the inventor of the steamboat, once drew an interesting analogy between language and invention: "The mechanic should sit among levers, screws, wedges, wheels, etc., like a poet among the letters of the alphabet considering them as the exhibition of tools in which a *new arrangement* transmits a new idea to the world."

The word *recombination* is important. Invariably, the raw materials for some new idea, or even for some new mechanical object, lie all around us. The process is simple. Old ideas combined with other old ideas produce new ideas. Not only that, but the basic principle of creative thinking claims that *quantity* breeds quality. To put it another way, the more new ideas we get, the better our chances will be of having good ideas. Here, again, we see the practice of deferred judgment. Being willing to live with some ambiguity is essential to a satisfactory finished product.

Occasionally in my classes I lay an ordinary building brick on the table in full view of the students. I then say to them: "Write on a piece of paper all the possible uses for this brick. Do not proliferate categorical uses, but specify different kinds of uses. That is, if you say the brick can be used for building, do not go on to say, 'for building houses, for building garages, for building walls,' etc. Building is one use."

Reactions to this assignment are usually interesting.

Some students attack the task enthusiastically and in just 10 or 15 minutes compile lists of 16, 18 or 20 uses for that brick. Others immediately become frustrated at the assignment and grumble at such foolishness in a college or seminary class. Still others start out with enthusiasm for the task but soon tire after locating in their minds only 2 or 3 uses that make sense to them. The problem that must be overcome in delineating uses for the brick is technically called *functional fixedness*, which means that we generally see only the standard use for an item (such as using a hammer only to hit nails).

Another hindrance to creative thinking is what is sometimes called *the incubation effect*. If ideation stagnates on a certain project, we might coax it back by putting that project aside and returning to it later. Perhaps during such an incubation period something inhibiting the solution loses its strength, and the solution can then occur.

Still another barrier to creative thinking is the old bugaboo of inhibition. We feel tied to concepts and behavior and have great difficulty breaking out of patterns to which we have become accustomed. This has a great deal to do with words. One mail order tool company had handled a product called "Crown Scissors," primarily used for dental work. In an attempt to increase the market for the item, the name was changed to "Bantam Tinsnips," and sales increased sharply. What had happened? The use of the item was largely dictated by its name—people had never thought of using "Crown Scissors" as tinsnips before!

What have we said in this chapter? Let's sum up by stating five axioms by which you can become a better leader by becoming a better thinker:

1. Practice the process of data gathering, always attempting to get as much information from as many sources as possible before making a decision.

2. Practice deferred judgment, waiting to make your decision until a good proportion of the evidence is in.

3. Practice lateral thinking by not always trying to walk in a straight line from your problem to possible solutions. This involves brainstorming unusual approaches to the problem.

4. Practice the "work aspects" of thinking in the expectation that you *can* become a more creative and positive thinker.

5. Practice creative thinking by projecting an unusual combination of or uses for ordinary materials or ideas.

CHAPTER

7

Can Your Colleagues Understand You?

T HROUGHOUT THE HISTORY OF THE WORLD, it seems that change has occurred slowly and that the world situation gives the appearance of being stable, almost immovable. But since 1900, the pace of change has increased dramatically. Kimball Wiles, college dean at the University of Florida, has pointed out that

> according to best estimates available, knowledge that has been accumulated prior to 1900 doubled in the fifty years after 1900, doubled again in the ten years between 1950 and 1960, and again in the seven years between 1960 and 1967. The rate of increase of knowledge is increasing so rapidly that it is estimated that by the year 2000 there will be two thousand times as many facts to know as there are at present.[15]

One of the basic responsibilities of leadership is to communicate adequate information to subordinates and supervisors. The inability to communicate has driven many a leader's ship upon the rocks of misunderstanding and bad information. The follower may be able to get away with the line, "I know what I want to say, but I can't explain it to you." Leaders, however, must not only know what they want to say, but they must be able to say it in a way that other people understand. Further, this responsibility focuses both on individual (eyeball to eyeball) and large group relationships when an explanation must be made, for example, in a public meeting. Until we become better communicators, we will not easily become better leaders.

Tearing down the barriers

William V. Haney is a professor at De Paul University and an industrial communications consultant. In his work with industrial managers, he has isolated 10 "semantic barriers" that cause difficulty in the communication process. Let us look at them within the framework of Christian leadership and, more specifically, within the ministry of a local church.

Bypassing. Communication is *meaning* exchange, not word exchange. To be clear about our communication we will expect people to look for the meanings to our words in *us*, not in the words themselves. The reverse is also true as we listen to other people attempt to explain things. Different words mean different things to different people. How about the Sunday school superintendent who told one of the teachers he would "drop by sometime next Friday afternoon to give you those materials." At one o'clock the teacher began to look for him only to wait until 5:30 for the arrival of the materials. The teacher had planned to work on them most of the afternoon, but the word *afternoon* meant one thing to the teacher and quite another to the superintendent. Bypassing is particularly common in talking about some abstract concepts difficult to visualize mentally. To really understand this point, try to describe a drawing or cartoon to someone else and have them sketch out a reproduction of what you have said.

Allness. We have a tendency to think we have exhausted

a subject after we have explained it to another person for 20 or 30 minutes. But no description of any object, idea or plan can cover all the details. Words become labels to tab the speaker's narrow view of the particular item he or she happens to be talking about at the moment. To keep the communication accurate, we should never expect that we have said all that might need to be said about a subject, or that we have heard all the "facts."

Guess Proneness. People tend to jump to a conclusion on the basis of the limited facts that they have about a given situation. This is true especially when we feel insecure or defensive about a particular problem. Sometimes the conclusions are valid on the basis of the information we have, but because of great gaps in that information, the conclusions are wrong in spite of their validity.

Hardening of the Categories. This is the simple problem of overgeneralization. Sometimes our subordinates seem alike because they happen to have some of the same generalized characteristics. We, therefore, forget their many individual differences and treat them all alike. Not only should we recognize their unique qualities, but we should attempt to develop those differences in order to create a broad base for ideas and flexibility in the organization.

Either/Or Thinking. People seem to have an innate compulsion to categorize things into boxes. Theologians are either liberal or fundamental. Churches are either large or small. Teachers are either good or bad. Such oversimplification does an injustice to the facts in a complicated world. Certainly some things are absolute, such as the sovereignty of God and the spiritual need of man. In terms of the biblical definition of *regeneration*, man is either a Christian or a non-Christian. But we cannot say that a man or a woman is either "spiritual" or "unspiritual." Growth in Christian maturity is much better depicted as a continuum rather than as a step from one box into another.

Blinderedness. Everyone knows that all churches should conduct an evangelistic campaign for two weeks every year. Or so we thought some years ago. For too long we allowed ourselves to be limited by the blinders of emphasis on special meetings. Now most churches recognize a variety of evangelistic methods—home Bible classes, coffee-shop ministries, friendship evangelism, to name a few. Perhaps the basic rule in overcoming this barrier could be stated this way: whenever you see only one way of doing something you should immediately look for another.

Thalamic Reaction. Some people spend most of their lives on the edge of a chair. Given just the right stimulus, they can spring off the chair and make some kind of decision on the basis of superficial information, using foolish examples to make the point. Here is a stereotyped example, but I think it gets the point across. A pastor was called on Tuesday morning and told that one of the Sunday school teachers had spent two hours in a local bar the evening before. In spite of the need for additional information, he immediately called the teacher and informed him that he would never teach again in that church. What the pastor did not know, however, was that those two hours had been spent in distribution of gospel tracts and sharing about Jesus Christ.

The *thalamus* is the sub-brain that receives basic stimuli. We do our real thinking with the *cortex*, or upper-brain. Unfortunately, we do not always let our ideas and communications go through that mental "Mayo clinic" before they emerge from our mouths. As a result, some are still as sick as when they entered the brain.

Misuse of Small Talk. Contrary to what we often think, the genial and casual nature of friendly conversation does not lend itself to the communication of important information and directives from the leader to his or her colleagues. We have a tendency not to take such items seriously because of the context in which we hear them.

Picture a young man handing his girlfriend a paper sack from the local grocery in which he has carelessly placed a diamond ring worth $750. Upon opening the sack she thinks it is all a good joke and concludes he probably bought his imitation glass diamond at the novelty store for a few cents. Paper sacks are fine for carrying groceries, but one expects a diamond ring to be properly encased in a velvet box with appropriate wrappings and ribbons. Goodwill and friendliness enhance relationships in leadership, but they do not always provide the context for discussion of plans, decisions and directives.

Misuse of "Is." General semanticists make a great deal of this issue. The simple word *is* has a connotation of unwarranted permanency. We tend to think that it applies to all situations—past, present and future. Consider the youth sponsor who complains to his pastor, "Greg Logan *is* just plain uncooperative. He won't listen in the youth meetings, he doesn't want to participate in projects, and he has no interest in anything we do with the young people." Both youth director and pastor tend to assume that the statement is fact, that Greg Logan possesses attributes that cause him to be uncooperative all of the time. As a matter of fact, the judgment is really "self-referential" in that the youth sponsor reflects himself in his analysis. Greg may or may not be like that, and if he is, the condition could persist only part of the time and in certain situations.

Misuse of "And." The word *and* is such a handy word. We use it in simple arithmetical settings to say, for example, "two *and* two equals four." We often fail to realize that the word carries much greater complexity, such as when we use it to say "man *and* wife."

Will Spaulding does a good job as the layperson in charge of visitation. It occupies more time than he felt he could really give to the work of his church, but it is an important ministry and God has blessed the organization and inspiration he has brought to the task. Because of his "success" with visitation, the pastor and the board asked him to assume additional responsibility, and he became "the layperson in charge of visitation *and* education." Such overwhelming dual responsibility brought abject discouragement within a year! Spaulding resigned his positions and lost all interest in working for Christ in the church because of his unhappy experience with the "visitation *and* education" overload.[16]

These basic communication problems stem from the nagging fact that we put too much emphasis on words and not enough on meaning.

How to be a good listener

G.K. Chesterton once remarked, "There is no such thing as an uninteresting subject; there are only uninterested people." How true that is when it comes to listening. Most leaders will spend more time listening than they will reading, writing or talking, but most are ineffective listeners. Communication specialists know that people in general tend to be poor listeners. They say, though, that listening, like leadership in general, can be learned.

The art of being a good listener will pay the leader dividends many times worth the original investment. A good listener can turn reaction to support by allowing the opposition to exhaust its arguments while he or she patiently and interestedly listens to all of them. In the process the listener increases his or her knowledge, develops an appreciation for the other person and position, and creates a climate of receptivity that encourages a continuing of the communication process.

Consider these five rules to better listening:

1. *Try to find something of interest and value to you.* Ability to search for hidden value in a conversation or lecture is a mark of maturity. Bad listeners mentally "turn off" a speaker and direct their attention to other, usually less helpful, functions. If we can make ourselves believe that a speaker has nothing of value to say to us, then we can quickly rationalize our inattention and say that we have not "learned anything" from the time invested.

In most listening situations, we are trapped anyhow, and we might as well put to use all of the brain power we can muster to catch something that can be put to good *use*. Sometimes it will be necessary to get around our emotional blockades to practice this kind of listening, but it can be done and it is the first step toward being a productive listener.

2. *Center your attention on content, not on delivery.* Many leaders find this extremely difficult to do, especially if they themselves are effective public speakers. The speaker's appearance, slavish following of the prepared manuscript or strange quirks of voice and bodily mannerisms trick us into thinking that he or she surely has nothing valuable to say. But remember that the key to listening requires minimizing qualities of presentation in order to find items of value.

3. *Concentrate on general ideas rather than on specific words or phrases.* Remember the definition earlier in this chapter: "communication is meaning exchange, not word exchange." Just because a speaker might not verbalize a certain concept exactly the way you might do it is no indication he or she does not have something important to

say about it. Poor listeners tend to listen for facts; good listeners capture principles. To put it another way, we achieve genuine learning better through understanding than through memorization.

4. *Stay flexible and open-minded while listening.* If all speeches and conversations were properly organized, listening would best be done by outlining the remarks of the speaker. Unfortunately, less than half of formal speeches and almost no informal conversations have an innate structure that can be followed. Listening, then, becomes the process of adapting to the way the speaker presents his or her ideas. Logical and progressive outline forms allow us to take notes in that way. When hearing a hodgepodge of ideas, however, we may have to grasp for key words or, better still, key ideas. Open-mindedness also requires that we do not "jump ship" if the speaker happens to use emotional language with which we may disagree.

5. *Discipline your mind to work at listening.* In our society adults soon learn to fake attention in any kind of public gathering. With a little bit of effort, we can even manage this in counseling or conversational situations. Such a lack of discipline betrays our disinterest in other people and exhibits a self-centeredness that can only lead to disaster in Christian leadership.

Although most of us spend more than 40 percent of the communication day listening to something, we tend to be inexperienced in handling different concepts and, like the 98-pound weakling who tries to lift a 150-pound weight, we buckle under the load and give up in weakness and frustration. If we realize that listening is an investment rather than an expenditure of time, we may be able to arm ourselves with the kind of "hard work" attitude necessary to develop good listening skills.

Above all, remember that communication is a two-way

street. Leaders are responsible to see that traffic flows smoothly in both directions. In listening to other people, leaders secure feedback that will enable them to adequately handle their responsibilities. In speaking, they must make sure that they have overcome barriers to good communication and that their colleagues understand what they are trying to say, even if they do not agree. Leaders must make their positions and ideas so clear that all members of the group have opportunity to agree or disagree on the basis of adequate and accurate information.

CHAPTER

8

Getting Along with People

SAM DECKER SERVES AS CHAIRMAN of the Christian Education Committee at First Church. As the purchasing agent for a local clothing chain, Sam seemed like a good candidate for that administrative position, because he is involved with leadership on his job. He has supervisory control over the activities of a small office staff, he makes executive decisions with respect to the expenditure of funds, and he has to involve himself with record keeping and reporting to the superiors of the organization. Further, Sam conscientiously reads up on trends and ideas in Christian education and has become an excellent resource person for the department.

But there is a problem. Sam has carried over to his work with the Christian Education Committee not only the positive functional aspects of his job but also the same crucial deficiency that has hampered his work at the office—Sam cannot get along with people. Making reports, drawing organizational charts and drafting plans pose no problem for him. But Sam is an administrator in both places, and *administration is helping people do things.* Eventually he will have to learn to work with others, or his success at work as well as his ministry for Christ in the church will be diminished.

The professional terminology for the content in this chapter is *human relations*. Management science experts emphasize that in business and industry human relations only provide a means to an end. If it ever becomes an end in itself, it ceases to serve the goals and functions of the organization.

If, for example, a man will turn out 17 pieces of work an hour if you pay no attention to him but 20 pieces an hour if superiors are nice to him, then the purposes of the organization are fostered when leaders are kind to subordinates. But many writers go on to say that when human relations becomes an end rather than a means, it is improperly used and has outlived its value for the organization.

Surely this is one point in which the church differs from a secular business organization. Jesus said, "By this all men will know that you are my disciples, if you love one another" (John 13:35). The maintenance of fellowship and community among God's people as they work together is one good example of an end in itself. It is also a means to an end. If teachers will be more effective, attend conferences more faithfully, study harder and teach better when their superintendent demonstrates human interest and concern in their lives as well as in their work, then human relations becomes a valuable tool. In the church, human relations is doubly important, because it is both a *means* and an *end* of much leadership activity.

Understand why people behave the way they do

In many ways the behavioral sciences are no friend of the biblical Christian. Much of what sociologists base their conclusions on is thoughtless evolutionary supposition, which completely ignores important theological factors such as the sinful nature of man, the redemptive power of God's grace and the work of the Holy Spirit in the individual Christian. Nevertheless, all truth is God's truth, and leaders ought to be on the lookout for insights and ideas that can come from a variety of sources, including research in behavioral science. The following three propositions have emerged from a great deal of study regarding the motivation of human behavior. You may note that they line up with several principles of Scripture.

People behave in accordance with the way they perceive themselves and their situations. This suggestion comes from the work of the "self-concept" psychologists who maintain that all people have some mental image of who they are and what they can do. The image may be accurate—that is, it may conform with reality—or it may be distorted. Which ever is the case, people do not act in accordance with reality but in accordance with the way they view themselves.

Have you ever asked someone in your church to take over a Sunday school class only to hear the response, "Who, me? I'm not a teacher; I can't teach." It is quite possible, of course, that the person was speaking the truth. On the other hand, that person may have developed a self-image that precludes in his or her mind the possibility that he or she could actually instruct a group of people in some given subject matter. Teacher training requires overcoming the negative attitude about self—that "early Moses syndrome."

People's perceptions are geared to preserve their pride and esteem. Some sociologists refer to this problem as "hiding mechanisms." Leaders are not immune to putting on a public face to cover up feelings of inadequacy or insecurity. This begins in the company of strangers whose motives are unknown and carries over into family and group relationships. This tendency to hide from one another results in a breakdown of communication lines and a failure to be open, human and personal.

Much of the older managerial research encourages leaders to remain aloof from their groups and sustain only the most formal and coldly cordial relationships with subordinates. No doubt this was to counteract any undue familiarity that could erode the authority of the leader's position. The human relations movement, however, captured again the spirit of the New Testament, particularly the words of Christ to His disciples: "I no longer call you servants, because a servant does not know his master's business. Instead, I have called you friends, for everything that I learned from my Father I have made known to you" (John 15:15).

Effective leaders, like Barnabas, encouraged people to retain self-esteem and increase what Abraham Maslow has called "self-actualization," while at the same time bringing perceptions of themselves into line with reality.

People sometimes maintain their esteem by rationalizing. Rationalization describes the attempt to attribute socially acceptable motives to our acts or words. We want people to like us even when we do something that seems to border on nonconformity. So we grope for the approval of the group or the agreement of the superior by claiming that the reasons for our behavior were actually good. Unless this becomes a pattern of life, it is probably quite harmless in incidental occurrence.

Leaders need to understand that people respond and react as they do because they see the action as consistent with their self-perceptions. When inconsistency raises its head, they quickly erase the problem by offering rationalization in an attempt to justify the act to the leader or to other members of the group.

Creating a climate for warm cooperation

Although leaders may not be held responsible for everything that goes on in an organization, they do have the responsibility for structuring a context for positive interpersonal relations. If an aura of distrust and hostility prevails in an adult class, for example, we look to the teacher who allows such a negative learning atmosphere to prevail. What kind of practical things can we do to keep people-relationships not only cordial but actually loving? The following principles may prove helpful:

1. *Understand people's needs.* No teacher can be effective unless he or she understands the generalized age-group characteristics as well as the specific local needs of the students in his or her class. In the same way, leaders have to know their people. Without prying into private lives, they should try to understand what kind of blessings and hurts their students carry that have an effect on their work. Such information comes from spending time with people in places other than the work or church setting.

2. *Know when and how to listen.* Although discussed in the last chapter, the various tasks of administration are so closely related that they clamor for attention here as well. Listening often proves therapeutic. It allows people to get problems "off their chest." Consider the Christian school principal confronted by an irate parent who stormed into his office one day complaining that her child had been unjustly punished by one of the teachers. For openers she shouted, "I want something done about this, and I want it done now!" Forty-five minutes later the closing remark was considerably more calm: "Thank you for taking time out of your busy day to listen to my complaint."

3. *Employ personnel policies that help people.* Too many personnel policies, even informal ones for church volunteers, tend to serve the interests of the organization instead of those of its people. We almost find ourselves in the position of saying, "If you keep our rules, we'll let you

work for us for nothing." God puts an enormous value on human beings. We know that because He sent His Son to die for them. But we often treat people like robots that exist for no purpose other than to carry out the goals of the organization in the way that we tell them to. Certainly in the Christian organization, kind treatment should be placed above administrative convenience in all policies and procedures dealing with personnel.

4. *Avoid passing the buck.* It is bad enough to pass the buck *up* when something goes wrong by pleading that we had nothing to do with a particular decision and by refusing to take responsibility for its consequences. It is much worse for a leader to hand the blame back *down* when something goes wrong. This human relations problem is as old as sin. Adam blamed Eve and Eve blamed the serpent. In a real sense, all were to blame, and Adam could have made an honest confession right at the outset by admitting that if he had proper spiritual control of himself and his family, the problem would never have occurred.

Willingness to take the blame and "keep the buck," comes when leaders are secure in their positions. Records of leadership and achievement must be sufficiently positive so that an occasional admission of failure will not endanger confidence in their ability to perform the task.

5. *Avoid manipulating people.* Exploitation of human resources is not Christian behavior even when we serve a supposedly good cause. Part of the secret to success here lies in the encouragement of cooperative efforts. If we can marshall people around the common cause of the organization while at the same time helping to meet their needs and developing their personalities, we service both "means" and "end" of human relations. Divisive vested interest should be discouraged if that can be done without destroying the initiative and enthusiasm of individual

workers. The self-discipline that comes from cooperative enterprise tends to result in a smooth-running team.

6. *Genuinely care about how people feel.* This step goes beyond understanding people's needs and attempting to fit their personalities to the organizational goals. Effective leaders remain sensitive to the feelings of their subordinates though they might not always agree with them. They can conduct a business meeting without arousing negative emotions. In conflict situations their sensitivity and alertness enable them to be aware of the reactions and feelings of everyone present, including those who have not entered the discussion.

7. *Never give orders that you know will not be followed.* Such a suggestion sounds like so much foolishness until we recognize that some leaders want to shout commands just for the sake of being recognized as commanders. They sound like parents berating their children with exaggerated threats, which they could not and would not carry out. Such a practice causes frustration in the family – and in the organization. Every time a worker fails to comply with a rule of the organization or an order from his or her superior, the potential for serious friction arises. This sticky situation can be averted if leaders will exercise proper discretion in issuing directives to their subordinates.

8. *Never blame or praise a group member publicly.* Of course, this is an overgeneralization. Frequently you will have occasion to offer some commendation publicly, and that may be a positive motivating force. Undue plaudits to a single member of the group, however, may lead other members to think that the leader "plays favorites" or thinks less of their work. On the other hand, public criticism will demoralize the organization immediately and

some members will suspiciously whisper in dark hallways, "I wonder who's next to get the ax."

9. *Use punishment in only the most extreme cases.* Too many leaders confuse discipline with punishment. Discipline means setting up fences or boundaries within which subordinates should function. Punishment comes when discipline breaks down and subordinates repeatedly climb over the fences and transgress the established boundaries. The wise leader designs conditions in which the group can discipline itself collectively. Individual violators become disenchanted with the standards of the organization and leave of their own choice.

Getting people to back your ideas

Part of human relations is the *means* aspect so important in business and industry. Leaders enlist people to support goals that they have originated or that have been handed to them by their superiors. A college dean must enlist the enthusiastic support of the faculty in achieving institutional goals that have been determined by the president and the board. Nonmanipulative motivation assumes that the leader sees the individual not only as a member of the organization but also as a person with needs and personality.

Generally speaking, people follow leaders who know where they are going. And, if leaders really want the wholehearted support of people, they should give them some voice in the organization and establishment of the program itself.

It also stands to reason that the leader has already enlisted the enthusiastic support of his or her superiors. For example, a director of Christian education about to launch a new program of teacher training must have complete pastoral backing if he or she expects to sell that program to the congregation. As feedback comes in from subordinates and superiors alike, various aspects of the program may have to be changed and brought into line with the wishes of other key people in the organization. There is a great deal of compromise in effective leadership. The final draft of any program or idea includes input from many sources up and down the chain of command.

It should be obvious that the program or idea under consideration has to be clearly mapped out in writing. Budget projections along with necessary personnel and facilities have to be carefully indicated on the write-up. Anyone questioning the workability of the plan can be shown that even though this kind of thing may not have been attempted before, all the known problems and options of how it will function have been thought through.

In their public presentation of the idea, leaders should act with enthusiasm and confidence. Like teaching, leading is often the process of exuding contagious enthusiasm.

Sometimes, even when all these steps have been followed and careful attention has been paid to the various facets of human relations, people still drag their feet. They often respond to reasons why the new program or idea will not work. Edgar Dale suggests that we ought to expect to hear several " 'good' reasons for doing nothing":

1. The new proposal might set a precedent.
2. We have not yet conclusively proved that the old method cannot be made to work.
3. This proposal is just another fad, which will pass in time.
4. The time is not ripe for this idea.
5. The situation is hopeless; why try anything.
6. We can't afford it.
7. This is a controversial issue.[17]

How can these objections be answered? Some of them are just foolish, and the irrationality of such reactionary thinking must be pointed out. For example, time never ripens. The ideas and mores of people change. Time has little to do with the value of an innovative concept. Other reactions must be answered rationally with objective facts and figures. If someone on the board suggests that "we *cannot* afford it," then it becomes the innovative leader's responsibility to demonstrate how the project *can* be afforded.

Still a third category of objections stems from ignorance that cannot be answered by either the proposer or the opposer because all speculations are hypothetical. Conceivably, any new way of doing things *may* be as bad as the old way. That is the risk we take with innovation. On the other hand, some ideas that look like fads at the beginning turn out to be established operating procedure—as the Wright brothers would be quick to testify.

People can easily become negative voices in the wilderness, and leaders hear many such voices shouting their doom. The impact of these voices, however, can be minimized and resistance can be changed to support, if we put proper emphasis on human relations and really work at getting along with people.

Leading Group Activities

T HE LAST DECADE HAS SEEN an emergence of the small
group within the evangelical church. Sometimes the
emphasis has been excessive, taking attention away from
the proper focus on the church. Most of the time, however, the small-group movement has sought to produce
individual and family renewal through the intimate interaction that small groups can afford.

Identifying the group

A group is a *gathering of individuals with common interests who are working and relating toward a common goal.* I
would offer the following five elements as the ingredients
necessary for a group's proper identification:

1. *Perceived unity.* People must recognize themselves as
a distinct identity in relationships.

2. *Common or shared goals.* These goals are usually
potentially rewarding, but the rewards may not always be
obvious to all of the group's members.

3. *Face-to-face interaction.* It is difficult to conceive of a
"group" in which the members never meet personally. The
essence of such interaction focuses attention on the nature of the group.

4. *Boundaries of participation.* Somebody has to be *in*
and somebody has to be *out* even though the boundaries

may be somewhat flexible and the group membership rather fluid.

5. *Organization.* This may be formal or informal. In the formal group there will be a chairman or leader and usually a secretary, treasurer and other officers. In the informal group the leadership will be emergent—different people may take charge at different times. But there will be general order based on a recognition of the group's objectives.

Most church groups meet for Bible study or for fellowship. As a leader, you obviously have contact with these kinds of groups, but you will give your attention more to the formally organized business group. Such groups take the form of boards, committees, small classes and informal gatherings of people for study and planning.

Throughout the Scriptures, group life and activity played a significant role. From Abraham's family to Isaiah's remnant, the Old Testament abounds with varying kinds and sizes of group activity.

The significance of groups

We live much of our lives in small-group interaction. The family is obviously the primary social group. Extending out from the home, the average person identifies with a number of other groups, some that are formal (such as employee unions, school classes and church boards) and others that are highly informal (such as a neighborhood womens' group that meets for coffee and dessert).

In your leadership role in the church, it is essential that you find (or help develop) a health and maturity in the groups you are involved with so that they see themselves functioning as a part of the total body of Christ. Every board or committee, every formal or informal gathering of people, which has as its purpose the facilitating of the work of Christ, ought to be representative of the unity and love of the whole body.

In these situations leaders must not become spiritual dictators who manipulate other people to their own ends. As a guide and coach they try to create a flexible and permissive atmosphere for listening, helping and, in general, drawing out the interests and potential of other members of the group.

Such was the role of Christ with the disciples and the role of the pastors and leaders in the early church. Peter warned first century church leaders not to lord it over "those entrusted to [them], but [be] examples to the flock" (1 Peter 5:3). This would enable them to work collectively in unity for the cause of the Savior.

The question of when a leader should use small groups was confronted and answered by Charles E. Hancock in an article printed in the Southern Baptist monthly publication, *Church Administration*.[18] According to Hancock, a leader should use small groups

1. *Whenever the demand for help exceeds the number, the time or the availability of those who can help.* Here Hancock draws a contrast between individual leadership techniques. The individual approach is not always possible and can be effectively replaced at times with the use of small groups.

2. *Whenever a group of people face similar issues.* A Sunday school superintendent, for example, who meets monthly with his 14 or 15 Sunday school teachers, leads people who face similar issues and problems. Their existence as a group meets all the definitions indicated above, and they feel secure in relating to one another in this kind of situation because of the homogenous nature of their tasks.

3. *Whenever it appears that individuals can help one an-*

other as much as (or more than) the leader can. The apostle
Paul told the Ephesians that the church should be mutually building itself up in a context of love. The properly
functioning group is a give-and-take situation in which the
members share themselves with the other members of the
group, giving and receiving information, challenge and
blessing for having been a part of the group.

4. *Whenever you need to measure or develop a person's
ability to relate to others.* Here the group is being used as a
training device. One's genuine attitudes and level of self-
control emerge more quickly in a small-group situation
than they otherwise would.

5. *When it is important to be intimate and to give everyone
a chance to participate.* Here the group becomes a form of
therapy, and we must not think of that word only in
relation to people who are ill. Hancock reminds us that
"there are groups of people who occasionally should get
off by themselves to deal intensively and exclusively with
one another without having to deal at the same time with
other people or issues."[19]

In the final analysis, the congregation itself is a group.
It will not always be a small group, although *small* is a
relative term. The communal nature of people in a local
church represents the unity of the Godhead and the spiritual oneness for which Christ prayed just before His death
(John 17:21). Reuel Howe once said that "in the past, the
church's primary emphasis has been on relationships between individuals. That emphasis is still important, but
now we must also develop the ministry of groups, utilizing
the group potential of the congregation itself."[20]

We must remember that the family, too, is a strategic
group. In fact, it is the most strategic group. The primary
purpose of marriage in God's sight is companionship between a man and a woman, as Genesis 2 clearly states. As

children are added to complete the family unit, the collective life of that group ought to be a primary concern of every local church. If at any time the church finds itself fragmenting instead of unifying the family group, its program stands opposed to the will of God. If the family group finds extension in a local church, then the emphasis on group harmony continues. The Bible teaches how the early Christians worked together with "one accord" (Acts 1:14; 2:1, 46; 4:24; 5:12; 15:25).

Group dynamics in the church

In the late 19th century and with increasing intensity in the 20th, the study of groups and leadership became a great concern of the developing social sciences. Today many research centers have been set up to study group dynamics. One can do graduate work at a number of universities with concentration in the area of group work and interpersonal relations.

A whole field of academic pursuit—the study of social psychology—concerns itself with the behavior of the individual within various kinds of social groups. Seminaries have discovered that unless they train students to make biblical content workable in the lives of people, their ministries will be frustrated (regardless of their knowledge of other areas).

We use the term *group dynamics* in at least four separate, but related ways. Some writers use it to describe the conflicting forces at work in all groups at all times. Others use it to describe a field of studies. Still others employ it to describe a body of basic knowledge about group behavior that has accumulated from research. For our purposes, however, we understand group dynamics as those forces inherent in the collective personalities of people in a group and as an analysis of how that potential can be unleashed to provide positive group life and productivity.

From a Christian point of view it is improper, and perhaps even impossible, to talk about group dynamics without a recognition of two biblical concepts: spiritual gifts and the personal ministry of the Holy Spirit. A leader working with a Christian group helps members place their thought process and ultimate behavior under the control of the Holy Spirit. Group dynamics are the inherent forces of collective personality. The leader does not create them; he or she serves as an instrument to direct or change them.

As people work together in group ministries, the collective exercise of their spiritual gifts causes the body of Christ to function. Only then can the church carry out its ministry in a communal way. Leaders must become skillful maestros conducting the symphony of God's grace. They do not beat their own drums or play several instruments. Instead they attempt to blend all the efforts of the orchestra into one harmonious sound, avoiding the discord and cacophony that so often distracts people from hearing the concert of faith.

In a healthy group the leader's role will be largely passive. He or she clearly has the authority of position—and perhaps the knowledge—but does not abuse that authority by turning it into authoritarianism. Dr. Grant Howard describes this kind of group leadership:

> If the leader acts as a boss, he plans, controls, directs, and decides. The group submits and conforms with passive assent. When the leader acts as a guide, he seeks to allow and to encourage the group to plan, control, direct, and decide. A guide is one who leads or directs another in any path or direction, showing the way by accompanying or going in advance. The

leader is to do just this. A string cannot be pushed, but it can be pulled. People cannot be driven, but they can be led. The leader functioning as a guide encourages and allows the group to formulate its own plans, to control and direct its own activities, to solve its own problems and to come to its own decisions. Then it is that the group will say of the leader: "We did this ourselves."[21]

If Howard is right, then the ultimate test of a leader's ability will be the mature, independent functioning of the group. As a leader you *will* work with groups. What is open to question is whether your groups will be sick groups or healthy ones.

Helping your groups be more effective through contrast

Perhaps the best way to analyze your present situation and plan for successful group leadership in the future is to notice several contrasts indicative of healthy and non-healthy groups. The first word in each contrast describes the healthy group; the second word represents the other end of the spectrum.

Effectiveness or attractiveness. Group *effectiveness* describes the extent to which groups generally reward their members. For example, if Sunday school teachers coming together once a month for staff meeting go home with information, inspiration and renewed enthusiasm for their teaching ministries, their group is effective. Group *attractiveness*, on the other hand, describes only the extent to which groups are expected to reward their members. *Attractiveness* is not wrong, but it becomes hollow activity if not followed by *effectiveness*.

Interaction or passivity. Interpersonal *interaction* is one of the most important elements of the healthy group. Research shows that people in a group who interact will change their behavior sooner than those who do not interact. *Interaction* also serves as postitive reinforcement, stimulating the group to further progress. *Passivity*, by contrast, describes a group in which members do not share with each other. Their unwillingness to share may be born of fear, or it may simply reflect their ignorance of group process. Whatever its cause, the leader must break down the inhibitions that prohibit effective *interaction*.

Process or content. A *process*-oriented group keeps one eye on the job to be done and another on the dynamics of the group. What happens to people as a result of working with the group is as important in a *process* group as the successful completion of the group's assigned task. The *content* group, on the other hand, ignores the feelings of its members toward one another, minimizes participation and, in its negative extreme, may even ride roughshod over the basic needs and interests of group members.

Security or insecurity. *Secure* group members accept their roles before God, feeling free to be themselves and to say what they think. They will not carry this freedom to extreme, injuring the sensitivity of other group members, but they are able to shed some of the "hiding mechanisms" that get in the way of interpersonal relations.

Insecure group members may participate in group work only to build or grasp status. They may care nothing for the other group members or for the basic tasks confronting the group. Their compulsion to dominate arises primarily from a basic *insecurity* and disenchantment with what they consider to be insignificant life roles.

Participation or control. Genuine involvement on the part of members is determined largely by the leadership style of the group leader. The so-called "great-man concept" of leadership will inhibit power and discourage *participation* because, after all, "the leader will do it." His or her *control* over the group may rest in iron-fisted dictation or in the positive charm of a spiritual godfather. The end result is the same—it becomes *the leader's* group, and the members hesitate to involve themselves in shared leadership.

On which side of the ledger do you find the groups in your church or organization? Do they show signs of maturity or immaturity? Of health or illness? Remember—the more mature the group, the less formal leadership needed. Be a coach and a guide. Let all the Indians share in the role of chief. The communal relations of God's people working together is a beautiful thing in His sight—and a powerful witness to the world.

You Can Speak in Public!

S OONER OR LATER, almost every leader will be faced with
the responsibility of giving a speech, a message or a
devotional talk of some kind before a public audience.
Many lay leaders in the church have had no preparation
for public speaking and face the task with great fear and
trembling. They take seriously the old tongue-in-cheek
remark, "A man's brain never stops functioning until he's
asked to speak." No less a man than Moses was ready to
throw in the leadership towel when told he would have to
speak in behalf of Jehovah.

Actually, most poor speaking does not come from a
deficient education in forensics or homiletics. We simply
violate basic principles that should be followed by every
speaker. These rules apply to the politician who addresses
a nationwide audience on television or to a high school
student fulfilling his first speech assignment by addressing
the class on the subject of how to water ski.

There are four elements to consider in public speaking:
the speaker, the audience, the speech and the Lord. If you
can relate to all of these—in preparation as well as in
presentation—you can do an acceptable job. That does not
mean that you will be an orator within a year, but people
will understand you, appreciate the effort you have put
into the speech and possibly even act objectively upon
your ideas.

The speaker: personality

A realistic view of your own abilities is essential to good public speaking. You should, for instance, decline some speaking invitations because you are not yet ready for that type of audience or because you cannot speak intelligently on the subject assigned.

One problem with public speaking is that we concentrate so heavily on what we *cannot* do that we tend to pass over what we *can* do. Start small. Speak to Sunday school classes or prepare a 5- to 10-minute devotional for a Sunday school worship time. Experience helps us gain confidence and poise in public speaking. Even the best speech classes in a respected university cannot provide the benefits of experience.

Another important factor is your attitude toward yourself and the speaking assignment. If you are afraid, that fear will be communicated nonverbally to your audience. Sometimes we suggest inadequacy with such opening lines as, "I really don't know why the pastor asked me to speak, because I don't know anything about the subject, but. . . ." or "I was only asked to do this last week, so I haven't had time to prepare, but. . . ." Starting a speech in this manner betrays insecurity and causes the audience to wonder if you really have anything important to say.

Do not forget the matter of appearance – the package in which your speech-gift is given. If the wrapping paper is all wrinkled and the ribbons soiled, people will tend to minimize the value of the gift, no matter how important it may be. Conservative clothing with moderate style-consciousness is always the best choice for the Christian leader, unless some unique kind of ministry requires a certain mode of dress.

In delivery of the speech, factors such as posture and

eye contact all play a part in securing positive results. If you use a pulpit or podium, do not lean on it or handle it unnecessarily. Stand erect but at ease, and above all, *look at the group as you speak.* When speaking to a small group (20–30), you will have ample opportunity to look everyone in the eye at some time during the course of your speech. In a large group, you may have to look at areas or glance at people as your eyes sweep across the room. What is *not* acceptable is to look at the ceiling, out the window, above the heads of the people or continually at your notes.

The audience: perspective

The better a speaker knows the audience, the more he or she will be able to adapt the speech to their interests and needs. Unfortunately, familiarity with the audience also carries a negative factor. Most speakers generally agree that it is more difficult to speak to an audience full of friends or family members. Consider the seminary student who has the responsibility of speaking in chapel or the Sunday school teacher who addresses his colleagues at the monthly workers' conference.

Dr. Walter L. Wilson, one of the most outstanding Bible conference speakers of the 20th century, was frequently asked to address groups—Rotary Clubs, Kiwanis Clubs and various other civic and service organizations—that would not normally be interested in Bible themes. Yet he was invariably received with great enthusiasm and invited back again and again.

His secret lay in determining ahead of time what kind of people would make up the audience and what subject matter would capture their attention and yet still be used as a vehicle to communicate the gospel. Sometimes his research would uncover notes of historical interest about the organization itself, things that even the members did not know. Occasionally he would do a "takeoff" on themes or mottos of the group—like the time he talked to a Kiwanis Club about the first Kiwanian, Nimrod, who built a city.

Understanding the audience does not mean everything you say will please them. Good speakers are not afraid of controversy, but on the other hand, they do not go out of their way to find it. Some nationally known speakers like to clear remarks that may be controversial with officials of the organization. If, for example, your views on a certain theological point disagree with those of the church in which you are scheduled to speak, you might want to tell the group in advance that you will offer another viewpoint on the subject.

This raises another important point relating to the audience. What objective do the leaders of the group have in mind for your speech? Are you being asked to come in as a supplier of information? Is this speech primarily for fund-raising or for motivating the group toward some particular project? What kind of decisions will be made as a result of your talk? These are things you have to know if you are to prepare properly and speak with clear-cut goals in mind.

The speech: presentation

Having something to say is a prerequisite to public speaking, but saying it properly is equally important. You can learn several simple steps in a brief time and then develop and polish them throughout your years of public speaking.

1. *Select your theme.* The theme might be a topic (a devotional talk on prayer) or it might be a text (Acts 1:8 as a challenge on witnessing). It should be apparent that theme selection depends upon your understanding of

yourself and the interests and needs of your audience. Be sure to speak on only *one* theme at a time, unless for some special occasion you have been asked to handle two different ideas in the same speech. The developing of one single thought will lend coherence and unity to your remarks.

Of course, it is important that the theme fit the objectives that the leaders of the group have set for you and the more specific objectives that you hope to accomplish as a speaker. In a real sense your preparation begins at the end rather than at the beginning. By delineating the objectives you hope to achieve, you can structure the content right on target. On some occasions you might want to clarify the objectives even before you select a theme. The kind of group and the occasion of the meeting will determine which comes first in your preparation.

2. *Develop your outline.* Arranging your talk into logical outline form is a major step in preparing an effective address. In an earlier chapter on communication, I noted that fewer than half of all public speeches have an adequate structure that lends itself to good listening and understanding. Acquiring skill in outlining takes time, but there are certain guidelines followed by the best speakers, and you can use them, too.

1. **Pattern.** The cliche, "three points and a poem" does not accurately portray good outlining, but it does come from the generalized principle that a good sermon or speech outline should be neither too short nor too long. One point is no outline at all, and seven or eight points will either take too long or require such scant coverage that the audience has only a vague concept of what you dealt with. Think in terms of no fewer than two and no more than five points in the structure of your address.

2. **Progress.** A speech should go somewhere from the beginning to the end. As the content unfolds, your listen-

ers should be able to see the direction you want to take them and thereby follow you to predetermined conclusions. In practice this means that each main point leads into the next, and all subpoints are logically arranged under the main points that they support.

3. **Parallelism.** Most outline points are difficult to follow because they do not have an inherent consistency that clearly marks them as related to one another. Following is a sample devotional talk from Philemon 4–7. The first outline takes nonparallel form; an improved version follows.

1. Paul's joy at Philemon's love and faith
2. Philemon's witness was to be effective
3. The saints enjoyed love

1. Reputation: Hopeful in the Lord (verses 4 and 5)
2. Communication: Faithful to the Lord (verse 6)
3. Consolation: Joyful for the Lord (verse 7)

If you were listening to this talk from Philemon, which of the outlines would you remember longer and follow more accurately? Parallelism means that word forms, such as nouns, verbs and adjectives, are used in the same place or position in each point phrase, clause or sentence. This particular outline has another literary device called *rhyming*. Good outlines do not have to rhyme, but they do have to be parallel. *Rhyming* simply means that the last syllables of one or more of the key words in the points are the same, such as *ation* in the sample above.

Another good literary technique to use is called *alliteration*. This is when consonant sounds, especially at the beginnings of words, are the same.

4. **Prominence.** The main points should highlight the kind of information that you talk about in the speech. For

example, if a speech entitled "How to Win Children to Christ" includes a point worded "faithful visitation," the content under that heading should give the audience information not about classroom activity or special evangelistic services, but about home visitation.

When you deal with biblical texts, let the outline emerge from the passage. Too many speakers try to superimpose a human structure upon a biblical passage when there may be an inherent logical form the Holy Spirit directed the writer to use. Here again, a practiced eye and many years of experience and work will enable you to see outlines in the Scripture so that you will teach it and preach it the way it was written.

Here are some other mechanical factors that will help in constructing a good outline: Be consistent in the numbering or lettering scheme you use. The following two examples are commonly used by professional speakers. Either one is acceptable if you maintain consistency of style throughout your outline.

I.
  A.
    1.
    2.
    3.
  B.

    C.
II.
  A.
  B.
  C.

I.
  IA.
    IA1.
    IA2.
    IA3.
  IB.

    IC.
II.
  IIA.
  IIB.
  IIC.

Also, keep your notes minimal, using only one side of one sheet of paper, if possible. This will protect you from staring at extensive notes and thereby losing eye contact with your audience. It will also force you to be more open to an informal style. If you have prepared well, the Holy Spirit can guide you in the use of specific words that will let you carefully cover the points you have delineated in your outline. I cannot emphasize too strongly that *the secret of speaking effectively with a brief outline is the quality of that outline.* You may never memorize a speech, but you can commit your outline to memory every time you speak.

Pay special attention to the introduction and conclusion. The introduction should capture attention and motivate people to want to hear what you have to say. The conclusion brings your thoughts to their culmination, drives home a significant application and tries to move your audience toward a decision about what you have said.

The Lord: power

When you have done all that you can and should do in preparation, you can still expect only mediocre spiritual results if your presentation is not empowered by the Spirit of God. He does not enter the picture at the end like frosting on the cake; you have to depend upon His leading throughout the entire process. Spread your notes before God (at least symbolically) and allow Him to take over your life, mind and mouth for the proclamation of truth. This applies not only when handling a biblical text or speaking to a Christian audience. All truth is God's truth. For the committed Christian, there is no distinction between secular and sacred aspects of life. If our lives are completely controlled by God, everything we do is of interest to Him, and we can depend upon Him to help in an employee motivational talk at the office as well as in teaching the Bible or in lecturing on theological themes.

Many things we have looked at in this chapter can be practiced apart from invitations to speak publicly. You should, for example, be constantly developing structural understandings of the Bible as you outline passages in systematic study. You could be collecting illustrations and topics so that when you are asked to speak, you will already have a file of resources to make preparation easier and more profitable. Then take every opportunity to speak, no matter how small the group or how insignificant the occasion may seem. Begin to build your confidence and work up a reservoir of experience until you realize the simple fact that you, too, can speak in public.

CHAPTER
11

When You Are in the Chair

EVERY LEADER WILL FACE THE JOB of conducting a formal business meeting. How he or she handles that task will reflect upon his or her leadership and will influence the ability of the organization to function properly. But many leaders dislike this aspect of their work, because they fear out-of-control meetings. The system does not cause the problems, however. More often than not, problems are caused by the incompetent or uninformed chairperson.

The most famous manual on parliamentary law is *Robert's Rules of Order*, first published by General Henry M. Robert in 1876. Three-quarters of a century later, the 75th anniversary edition found greater popularity than any of the previous printings. In the Preface, Robert defines his objectives:

> The object of *Rules of Order* is to assist an assembly to accomplish in the best possible manner the work for which it was designed. To do this it is necessary to restrain the individual somewhat, as the right of an individual, in any community, to do what he pleases, is incompatible with the interests as a whole. When there is no law, but every man does what is right in his own eyes, there is the least of real liberty. Experience has shown the importance of definiteness in the law;

103

and in this country where customs are slightly established and published manuals of parliamentary practice so conflicting, no society should attempt to conduct business without having adopted some work
upon the subject as the authority in all cases not cov-
ered by its own special rules.[22]

Churches have been split, thousands of people offended
and great organizational problems created simply because
somebody did not know how to lead a meeting properly.
Yet you do not have to be a professional parliamentarian to
conduct business affairs in a decent and orderly fashion. If
Robert's manual seems too difficult, find other more sim-
plified devices. This chapter provides 10 helpful guidelines, which you may follow when it becomes your responsibility to conduct a formal business meeting.

Recognize the values of committee work

Our informal society causes many church leaders to
react negatively to organization and formal administrative
practice. One of the first things to be attacked is the
system of boards and committees that seems to them to be
mercilessly slow at best and a training ground for anarchy
at worst. Foolish slogans have arisen, such as "God works
through people not committees," as though somehow people in groups cannot be led by the Holy Spirit!

As a matter of fact, the New Testament provides signifi-
cantly greater evidence that God works through people in
groups more than He does through individuals. This is
particularly obvious in the New Testament church in the
Book of Acts. In one of my larger books on leadership, I
attempted a defense of the board-and-committee system:

The values of committee work should be obvious. Certainly the significance of group ideation is greater than

the thought processes of one man attempting to solve a problem. Second, in Christian circles the fellowship of God's people working together to accomplish God's work in God's way should make committee activity a monthly highlight for church educational leaders. Third, the presentation of joint thinking on a controversial issue has more authority and can develop more respect than the attitude of one individual, even if he is the Pastor or Director of Christian Education. It is high time in the organizational patterns of the evangelical church for us to stop throwing stones at the utilization of committees and recognize instead the great contributions they can make toward achieving the objectives that the local church sets out to accomplish.[23]

Know the difference between boards and committees

Generally speaking, a committee serves under and in connection with a board. Committees study, discuss, evaluate and recommend. Boards set policy to be carried out by administrators. Of course, it is also possible for a board to delegate some of its policy-making activity to a duly appointed committee.

In some organizations the words are used almost interchangeably. There is probably not much danger in that as long as leaders know the respective role of each group. Boards usually take a broader picture of the organization; committees focus on a particular area of a problem or need. For example, the official board of a local church might have committees on finance, missions and pulpit ministry, among other things. Committees can also have subcommittees—a church committee on Christian education might choose to appoint subcommittees on Vacation

Bible School, leadership training, plant and facilities and music education.

Obviously the more subcommittees an organization develops, the more bureaucratic it becomes. But let us not forget that some evidence of bureaucracy only indicates formal functioning of the organization. Most professional management writers indicate that bureaucracy, in itself, is not wrong—only the excess and misuse of bureaucratic operations tend to corrupt the organization. Do not feel then that if your church has a board, several committees and even some subcommittees, it is getting hopelessly entwined by the damp, dark cords of bureaucracy.

Plan the agenda carefully

Let us assume that you will chair the business section. It will be your responsibility to set up the meeting and to prepare board or committee members for their collective tasks. The first step in carrying out a successful meeting is the planning of an agenda. The agenda should be written *in advance* and copies distributed to all members. Depending on how frequently the group meets, "advance" might mean several hours or as much as a week. This will give them some idea of what will be discussed and what kind of preparation they should make to attend and participate intelligently.

Also, the agenda should specify the actions that need to be taken. Rather than just indicating that plans for the new educational unit will be discussed, for example, you might want to say, "Discussion of bids on new educational unit and selection of the most satisfactory proposal." This kind of detailing will prevent an absentee committee member from saying after the meeting, "Oh, I thought you were just going to talk about the new building some more. If I had known you were really going to make an important decision like that, I would have come." This is all part of the strategic task of communication, and *the leader must exert his or her best efforts to keep members properly informed at all times.*

Preside with a good view of your leadership role

It is difficult to be presiding officer, particularly if you are already the acknowledged leader of the organization. *For this reason many churches have decided that it is unwise for the pastor to be moderator or chairman of formal business sessions.* Because of his acknowledged leadership, it is difficult to maintain a neutral role in conducting the affairs of the organization. Almost everything he says will be interpreted as an attitude for or against some business matter, causing him to sway votes without even meaning to.

In his helpful book, *When You Preside,* Sidney Sutherland indicates that the presiding officer of a business meeting has five basic responsibilities:

1. To *initiate* items or proposals for the members to consider; to bring before the group matters on which they may wish to take action.
2. To *facilitate* the deliberations and actions of the group; to make it easier for them to conduct the business that has brought them together.
3. To *orient* and guide the group in the conduct of their business.
4. To *encourage* and bring about a free and complete discussion of matters brought before the meeting; to act as a harmonizer when debate waxes a little too warm.
5. To *summarize,* clarify, and restate motions made and considered by the group prior to voting.[24]

Carrying out these five tasks with cool competence is

no small responsibility. It requires a strong democratic view of leadership to avoid the fear of group manipulation. The old adage, "power corrupts," seems just as true in the small Christian organization as in a national bureaucracy. If you really see leadership as service to the group, then you will work to facilitate the achievement of group goals and not to superimpose your views and biases upon the people voting in the business meeting.

Allow all issues to have fair hearing

The role of chairperson becomes a "sticky wicket" when controversy arises. Factions may develop in the group, and each side tends to think that the chair favors the opposing viewpoint. Sometimes you may want to measure equality so closely you actually use a stopwatch to time the speeches supporting or condemning certain motions. If you do this, appoint a neutral timekeeper rather than handling it yourself. You need all your attention and energy to skillfully keep the discussion on a positive level and to balance the opportunities for presentation demanded by all people involved.

Know the constitution and bylaws of your organization

Business affairs are conducted slovenly at best—and illegally at worst—when the chair or presiding officer does not know the legal processes of the organization. The constitution and bylaws should be current and available at all times. Copies should be placed in the hands of every member of the board or committee so that every decision affecting the future of the organization can be made in accordance with proper procedure. If no one else has a copy of the constitution at a business meeting, make sure you do, so you can refer to it if any questions arise.

Perhaps this problem can best be seen by looking at an example, the matter of nominations. Nominations can be made in three ways: by the assembly, by nominating committee or by ballot. It makes a great deal of difference which one you use, because your constitution probably specifies how certain officers are to be nominated. Usually that document will also spell out how the nominating committee comes into existence. Is it appointed by the chair? Elected by the assembly? Does the assembly have the right to insert further nominations after the nominating committee presents its report? These matters are not decided at the moment if there is some constitutional base.

And what about the questions of majority or plurality? May anyone vote in this particular election or must he or she be a member in good standing by virtue of having paid certain dues or attended a certain number of meetings of the group within the past year? These are important questions. If the bylaws have nothing to say, then you may decide at the point of motion how these matters will be conducted.

Keep accurate records and reports

The official records of a business session are called "minutes." They keep an account of proceedings and may be corrected at any time without reconsidering the vote that approved them. Minutes should include all main motions but may exclude motions that were withdrawn.

Points of order, appeals and other significant motions that are not withdrawn should also be recorded. Official minutes often include the hour of meeting, the time of adjournment and the name of primary movers as well as a list of those members of the roll present at the business session. Even when the name of the mover is recorded, the name of the seconder is generally not included.

Minutes should be kept of all regular and all special meetings. Sometimes you may want to include such items as the name of the presiding officer, the motion for approval of minutes of the last session and a summary of reports given by officers in the organization.

Here are three simple ways to cut down on the bulk of minutes, making them more readable and useful.

1. *Use the code MSC to indicate that a certain action was "moved, seconded and carried."* This eliminates all the verbiage leading into each motion and enables a reader to see at a glance whether or not a motion carried. Obviously, if the motion was defeated only M and S appear. Remember that a motion has to have a second to be valid at all, so the symbol M would never be used alone.

2. *List actions in abbreviated form on the first page of the minutes.* For some important meetings, the minutes may go on for several pages. In a case like that it may be wise to list significant motions on the first page. Here is a sample of what that might look like in the minutes of a church Christian education committee:

1. Mary Simons appointed director of Vacation Bible School for next summer (page 2).
2. Missions education committee appointed to include Bill Harmon, Sam Reider and Martha Glocken (page 2).
3. Seventy-five dollars budgeted for the improvement of the leadership section of the church library (page 3).
4. Approval given to the Sunday school staff for the planning of a spring Sunday school picnic on May 4 (page 3).

5. Two new workers approved for service in boys' club program: Al Crandle and Mack White (page 4).

Obviously, the official details of each action would appear on the page indicated in the parenthesis. Listing them this way enables anyone to see at a glance the kind of significant actions that were taken at any given business meeting.

3. *Use a numbering system for actions.* If you start with one and carry the process through for the life of the organization, you will have a complete record of all the actions and can refer to former actions by number. This will save a lot of space in future minutes. For example, rather than referring back to a certain action about VBS dates, you can just refer to that as action 376. Any person having a complete set of minutes can then trace back to see what action 376 is all about and under what circumstances it was carried and implemented.

Be careful of the problem committee member

Invariably you will encounter members of the group who seem to impede rather than enhance progress. The *spectators*, for example, never have anything to say. They contribute little to the group and offer no input on other people's suggestions, much less any creative suggestions of their own.

On the opposite end of the line are the *monopolizers*, who want to take all the group's time to air their own views. As chairman you may have to exercise your leadership prerogative and "turn them off" so that the meeting can move on.

Many groups also have *company clowns* who waste time in the business meeting by wisecracks and smart remarks.

Their problem usually stems from insecurity, which they attempt to cover up by spreading the entire business meeting with a veneer of humor.

Perhaps the most dangerous of negative group members are the *manipulators*. These people know the process of conditioning and attempt to swing the group's vote their direction by applying the proper words at the proper time.

As a leader you have the responsibility to neutralize the influence of negative group members and make sure the group presses toward its assigned goals.

Use proper language in meetings and reports

Leaders are teachers, and in the context of a business meeting you need to teach your group members how to speak correctly. When a group member offers a motion, he or she should not say, "I make a motion," but rather "I move." Terminology such as "point of order," "rescind and expunge," and "accept or receive" should soon be the working vocabulary of your group. Do not let group members make a joke of serious business. Although the experience of carrying on business does not have to be stern and puritanical, the opposite extreme is also unfortunate.

Conduct business in accordance with proper rules of order and parliamentary procedure

No doubt this will be an area in which you will need further information. Several books are helpful, starting, of course, with *Robert's Rules of Order*. You might also want to take a look at *Parliamentary Law at a Glance* by E.C. Utter (Reilly and Lee Company). Other helpful sources are *The Meeting Will Come to Order* by Harold Sponberg (Michigan State University, Extension Bulletin No. 294), and *A Guide to Parliamentary Practices* by Melvin Henderson and Herbert J. Rucker (The Interstate Printers and Publishers, Inc., 19 N. Jackson Street, Danville, IL). The following chart taken from Sidney Sutherland's book, *When You Preside*, will help you in parliamentary procedure:

TABLE AND RANK OF MOTIONS

MOTION	In order when another speaker has the floor	Requires a second	Debatable	Amendable	Vote Required
1. Fix time to adjourn or for next meeting	No	Yes	No	Yes	Maj.
2. Adjourn	No	Yes	No	No	Maj.
3. Take a recess	No	Yes	No	Yes	Maj.
4. Point of privilege	Yes	No	No	No	None
5. Call for the orders of the day	Yes	No	No	No	None
SUBSIDIARY					
6. Lay on the table	No	Yes	No	No	Maj.
7. Previous question (close debate)	No	Yes	No	No	Two thirds
8. Limit-extend debate	No	Yes	No	Yes	Two-thirds
9. Postpone to a definite time	No	Yes	Yes	Yes	Maj.
(Special Order)	No	Yes	Yes	Yes	Two-thirds
10. Refer to a committee	No	Yes	Yes	Yes	Maj.
11. Amendment to the main motion	No	Yes	Yes	Yes	Maj.
12. Postpone indefinitely	No	Yes	Yes	No	Maj.
INCIDENTAL					
A. Point of order	Yes	No	No	No	None
B. Appeal to the chair	Yes	Yes	Yes	No	Maj.
C. Parliamentary inquiry	Yes	No	No	No	None
D. Point of information	Yes	No	No	No	None
E. Division of Assembly	Yes	No	No	No	None
F. Close nominations	No	Yes	No	Yes	Two-thirds
G. Re-open nominations	No	Yes	No	Yes	Maj.
H. Method of voting	No	Yes	No	Yes	Maj.
I. Request to withdraw a motion	No	No	No	No	Maj.
J. Suspension of rules	No	Yes	No	No	Two-thirds
K. Objection to consideration of a question	Yes	No	No	No	Two-thirds
RENEWAL					
L. Reconsider	Yes	Yes	Yes	No	Maj.
M. Take from table	No	Yes	No	No	Maj.
N. Repeal or rescind	No	Yes	Yes	Yes	Two-thirds
O. Discharge a committee	No	Yes	Yes	Yes	Two-thirds
MAIN MOTION	No	Yes	Yes	Yes	Maj.

Reprinted from *When You Preside* by Sidney Sutherland, published by The Interstate Printers and Publishers, Inc., Danville, Illinois. Copyright 1962. Used by permission.

12

How to Change Things
(And Live to Tell about It)

A PASTOR IN THE MIDWEST has a plaque sitting on his desk that says, "Come weal or come woe, my status is quo." That caustic motto represents the attitude of many people in the church today, and that attitude makes our work as leaders more difficult to perform. Let's face it, change comes slowly and carefully in the evangelical church, which in most respects is good—we never want to change the timeless truths of our faith, only make them relevant to today's believer.

Nevertheless, leaders are responsibile to initiate improvement, and that necessitates innovation. In *The Change Masters*, Rosabeth Moss Kanter—one of America's leading authorities on corporate innovation—lists 10 surefire ways a manager can stifle innovation:

1. Regard any new ideas from below with suspicion.
2. Insist that the people who need your approval first go through several other levels of management.
3. Get departments/individuals to challenge each others' proposals.
4. Express criticism freely; withhold praise; instill job insecurity.

    5. Treat identification of problems as signs of failure.
    6. Control everything carefully. Count everything in sight—frequently.
    7. Make decisions in secret and spring them on people.
    8. Do not hand out information to managers freely.
    9. Get lower-level managers to implement your threatening decisions.
   10. Above all, never forget that you already know everything important about the business.[25]

Why do people find change difficult?

Frustration and confusion brought about by organizational change present a genuine problem for people. Most of us like things the way they are even though we may complain about them. Change poses the threat of the unknown—that dark, dismal tunnel with nothing but question marks at the other end. But there are also pragmatic reasons why people resist change. The following list is not exhaustive, but it does indicate some of the roadblocks faced in trying to bring about new ways of doing things:

It is easier to do what we have been doing. Change shakes the bushes and rips up the rugs. When the sacred cows lie dying along the river of progress, their owners will surely seek vengeance on the innovator who slew them. There is also the issue of retraining for the new way: "I know what I am doing the way I am doing it, but if I start to do it the way you want me to do it, I will be confused and frustrated because I do not know that pattern. Can I not learn it? Of course I can, in time. But that will require effort on my part, which I would not have to expend if we continued doing it the old way."

Doing things the new way might lead to failure. Most

failures that human beings experience happen when they are trying to do something for the first time. Consider the little boy who falls while trying to ride his new bicycle. Even though he scraped his arms and knees, he keeps at it for only one reason—the motivation of being able to ride. In most organizational change that kind of motivation is not built in, and all people can see is the immediate spectre of failure. Benefits of change are not always clear, sometimes even to those who have to work the hardest to bring it about; so resistance seems natural.

We often misunderstand what the change is all about. The motto of negative church membership is simple: "If you don't understand it, oppose it." A director of Christian education, for example, may clearly explain why a short-term summer missionary trip would be good for the senior high youth group. But unless parents can grasp why it can be a good and productive idea for their teenagers, they may refuse to support it and thus effectively kill its usefulness.

Change stirs our feelings of loneliness and insecurity. People have strong emotional attachments to ideas and to other people. A church calling a new pastor may discover some members voting against a certain candidate just because other members voted for him. Moments of major change are moments of crisis; when feelings of inadequacy surface, people sometimes try to cover those feelings by fighting the threat that stirred them up.

Some people have a greater problem with this than others have. It may be related to the security that a person feels in his or her family relationships, job, positions at church and general role in society. If the foundations rock in any one area, it could carry over to other areas. Other people will feel the tremors, because a person will involuntarily carry along the frustration.

Essential ingredients for positive change

When you find it is your responsibility to initiate change (and as a leader you will be doing this quite frequently), you can facilitate the process by "plugging in" several elements that management research has isolated as crucial to successful change. What are some of these elements?

Association. The association that people sustain with others in the work group determines their acceptance of (or resistance to) change. The more narrow one's associations, the more limited the frame of reference and the more likely he or she will be to fight new forms. In order to create a climate of change, you will want to broaden the contacts and associations of the people in your group.

Involvement. One of the major postulates of motivation recognizes that people participate more energetically in a project if we involve them in its planning. As a leader you will be hovering on the brink of disaster when you hand down ideas and projects from your drawing board and then ask people to make them work at the grass-roots level. Develop dialogue and interaction among the members of the group so they have a significant voice in structuring the change as well as living with it after it happens.

Relationship. In a counseling situation, we overcome resistance and fear by building up a trust relationship. Organizational change operates much the same. If your people already show a bit of distrust in the way you run things, the more changes you introduce, the more threatened they will become (and the quicker you will lose your job). I have often told my students that when they come to a new ministry, they should "change nothing major the first year."

Sometimes that warning itself introduces a problem

because people want to see "results" in the ministry of their leaders. The danger in our day, however, seems to be overdoing it rather than adopting a policy of laziness. *First build trust and confidence in your leadership*; then talk about change.

Commitment. Too often we bring people into the act *ex post facto.* That is, after the leaders have decided what they want done and how to go about doing it, they brace themselves for what they know will be great difficulty in selling the plan to the constituents. The principle of commitment suggests that we solicit meaningful involvement in the project as early as possible. People should say *our* class, not *your* class; *our* church, not *your* church. In bringing about change, leadership is the process of *working with people*, not *working over them*, or worse yet, *working them over*.

Steps in the process

We have looked at why people resist change and what basic ingredients generally characterize successful innovation. Now let us put it together by delineating five steps or techniques that can be used to manage change.

1. *Make plain how the change facilitates organizational goals.* Assuming your people clearly understand the objectives of the organization (and that may be a major assumption), any change in the functions or form of the organization should relate back to the stated objectives. The educational cycle requires constant evaluating on the basis of educational objectives. Conceivably, the objectives might change, or more commonly, our understanding of how the objectives may be best achieved will change. Such a reevaluation may require restructuring in the organization. Evidence shows that *people change more rapidly, with more positive results, when they understand how any innova-*

tion enhances rather than obscures the fulfillment of purposes with which they are in agreement.

2. *Create a positive climate for change.* Many leaders run into difficulty in the process of change primarily because they stand up to bat with two strikes against them. Hostility and dissatisfaction pervade the organization, and the announcement of change simply offers the *coup de grace* in that leadership union. Such confusion leads to "bargaining," a poor substitute for a happy climate in the organization.

Three factors can help create a positive climate. The first is the process of "unfreezing." This term is applied primarily to the creation of dissatisfaction with the status quo. To put it more simply, people have to be somewhat unhappy with the present situation before they will entertain the virtues of change. In the church, "God's frozen people" have to be thawed a bit, and as with most thawing processes, this one is accomplished through warmth.

A second significant factor is the maintenance of a nonjudgmental attitude on the part of the leader. Leaders are human, too, and they have just as much tendency as the next person to react negatively when someone opposes their plans or programs. But such a "cold" attitude can never facilitate the thawing process. Condemnation can change common ice cubes into dry ice, and the whole prospect of change will be doomed.

Still a third facet of climate creation is the building of a base of support or, if you please, lobbying. Too many leaders try to win their battles on the floor of the committee or board. They operate with a "William Jennings Bryan complex," thinking that pure democracy demands open oratorical defense of every issue. But sometimes things do not get done that way.

Our Lord, for example, was constantly "lobbying" with

His disciples. He would plant pieces of information and seed-thoughts for ideas that He hoped would blossom and come to fruition in a future day. This is precisely what the leader does when he or she meets directly with key people in the organization.

3. *Involve a maximum number of people at all levels in the change process.* Isolated group members have limited effect working by themselves. Research shows that one of the best ways to obtain group cooperation is to let people have a larger "piece of the action." Sometimes we call this "decentralization." Some managers go so far as to say that the best thing you can do with a new idea is to separate it from the leader who first had it and to make it group property.

In the same way groups set up the machinery to thwart change, they can provide the wherewithal to facilitate it. The trick is to get as many people on your side of the net as possible before the match begins. The extent to which such a participation emphasis will work depends upon the sincerity and honesty with which you go about involving other people. This is not tokenism, but rather a genuine commitment to a democratic leadership style.

4. *Begin at the point of most control.* This is a time-honored principle of change. Some leaders go awry because they try to reach beyond their area of control to produce innovative procedures. It is easier to speak to a man who is close to you than it is to shout at someone a quarter mile away. All leaders have a particular reference point of authority. A Sunday school superintendent, for example, who wants to see genuine renewal in the church, would be unwise to start recommending changes in the deacon board or the missions program. He or she should begin with the Sunday school—his or her point of most control. Leaders must examine their own situation to

determine what parts of the change most closely relate to areas of their authority.

5. *Begin at the point of most predictable results.* As indicated earlier in this chapter, fear of the unknown is one of the major problems with change. Even leaders find it hard to foresee all the implications of major change. But we should make every effort to predict what will happen when the machinery of innovation begins to crank.

Some years ago, as dean of a small college, it was my responsibility to design and introduce an entirely new curriculum plan. One of the most significant aspects of the planning was to brainstorm the possible problems we might encounter upon implementation of the new program. When we actually set it in motion, many things emerged that we had not, and probably could not have, predicted. Nonetheless, we had at least made an effort to determine what direction things would go.

It is difficult to conceive of a situation in which no prognostications could be made about the results of a change. In your planning procedure, analyze points of predictability and implement change first in an area in which you have maximal reliabilty.

Machiavelli once said, "There is nothing more difficult to take in hand or perilous to conduct, or more uncertain in its success, than taking the lead in the introduction of new things." Machiavelli is hardly a model of Christian leadership, but it so happens that in this analysis he was right. Resistance to change can be minimized and the negative foe conquered if you proceed carefully. A leader can bring about change—and still live to tell about it!

13

Committing Your
Leadership to Others

L EADERSHIP SHOULD BE LIKE a contagious disease. Everyone who comes in contact with you while you have it
should catch it to some degree. Of course, there is one
major difference: when you have a disease, you deliberately try to avoid giving it to anyone else. Here you will
want to parcel out leadership as rapidly as your group
members qualify to accept it.

Paul speaks of the contagion in Second Timothy: "For
you must teach others those things you . . . have heard me
speak about. Teach these great truths to trustworthy men
who will, in turn, pass them on to others" (2:2, LB). Because of his or her salvation experience, a Christian ought
to be able to tell other people how to become Christians.
In somewhat the same manner, a leader should be able to
share leadership with others who can carry on the chain
of command. One of the curses that follow in the wake of
one-man leadership is the vacuum created by the super-
star's inability or disinterest in developing subordinate
leadership.

Finding the person

Where is your Timothy? Where is your Silas? Where is
your Priscilla? Where is the promising leader who is learn-

ing how to take responsibility in the organization by watching you? That person may be a teacher or an assistant Sunday school superintendent. He or she may be a departmental superintendent or a girls' club worker. Roles and abilities differ widely, but somewhere in your church or organization is a person or group of people whom you should be tailoring either for your mantle or for similar garments of leadership.

But why is finding leadership in local churches so difficult? That question can be answered by saying that leadership problems usually fall into one of two categories: spiritual or organizational. Either category could be affecting the recruiter as much as the potential worker. A spiritual problem is a problem of heart and life that gets in the way of God's clear call for service. It might be an improper motivation or a lack of dedication. It may be sin or stubbornness hindering the Holy Spirit's leading. Organizational problems commonly stem from improper handling of personnel recruitment.

One aspect of the organizational problem is that we do not really know "who is out there" or what they can do. Periodic reporting becomes essential to improve recruitment. Dr. Roy B. Zuck suggests that you should

> Canvas your church membership annually using a printed or mimeographed form on which the people are asked to state their past experiences in church educational ministries, present experiences and responsibilities, and the agency and age group they would like to serve either immediately or in the future. When asking the people to complete the form (at a church service or elsewhere), state the purpose of the procedure and stress the importance of those *spiritual* ministries.[26]

Perhaps the nature of your work as a leader will require spending time in mass recruitment. It will at least demand a focus on the whole organization and its personnel needs. In doing this, however, do not lose sight of the Paul-Timothy concept and the significance of finding a man or woman to whom you can personally relate as teacher to disciple by building your life into that person.

Measuring ability

How can you tell whether or not a potential worker really fits the task? What is the margin of risk that this person will not perform satisfactorily and create more problems for the organization? This question is faced whether appointing a new custodian or a new pastor. Every time the Christian education committee decides upon teachers for the coming year or fills a vacancy in the educational program, they have to ask about ability, evaluation and assessment.

Ted Engstrom and Edward Dayton, in *Christian Leadership Letter*, observe,

> [It is hoped that] you will be able to find more than one applicant for the job. If this is the case, go through the various applications and other information that you have, and decide from what you read which ones you would like to talk to first. If the person does not have to travel far for an interview, it's best to set up an initial screening time in which you can get an overall feel as to whether you think it worthwhile to set up interviews with . . . other people. If the person is coming from a distance, then do some personal screening on the telephone.[27]

It is important to point out that you will frequently be looking for the potential or the capability to develop leadership gifts and attitudes, not the professional exercise of leadership skills. This is true particularly in working with lay people in the local church.

Here are some questions used by the American Association of School Administrators in looking for administrative leaders, such as superintendents, principals and the directors of various programs. The questions have been modified somewhat to fit the perspective of local-church leadership.

1. Is the potential leader's reputation as a person and as a worker respected by other members of his or her work group?
2. Does the person have sufficient aggressiveness and enthusiasm to promote the program for which he or she is under consideration?
3. Does the person have personal courage exercised with appropriate tact in facing opposition and in dealing with quarrelsome subordinates?
4. Is the potential leader a creative person who can provide fresh, innovative ideas for the organization?
5. Is the candidate a genuine Christian who understands the meaning of prayer and who knows how to study the Bible for him or herself?

Recruiting for leadership

One major industrial corporation has a brief and interesting motto for its personnel department: "Seek the ideal—Settle for the practical!" This company recognizes that no candidate for a leadership position will be superior on all counts. They aim, then, for the best combination of positive attributes. Of course, this is even more true in the selection of lay leaders for the local church. Just because there are fewer candidates to pick from, however, does not minimize the importance of the task. In fact, *minimizing* the standards of excellence in local-church leadership contributes to the problem of worker recruitment. Not many people want to work for a shoddy organization.

Sometimes a leader thinks it is difficult to recruit volunteer workers: "Wouldn't it be much more effective if we could offer salaries to people for leadership positions?" Yet it is interesting (and encouraging) that business and industry are doing more and more with nonmonetary incentives. They have discovered that people work for reasons other than wages and bonuses.

Training for the job

Once the new leader has been located and recruited, he or she becomes a member of the team. It is necessary to teach that person how to play your kind of ball game, using your signals and your plays, so he or she will not have to spend all the time on the bench. It is precisely at this point that many leaders make a mistake in recruitment. They work hard on prospects until they give a "yes" answer and then rush off to some other task, leaving them to find out for themselves what they are supposed to do and how they are supposed to do it.

It is impossible in the few pages of this manual on leadership to delineate all the aspects involved in a thorough training program. There are three specific elements, however, that should form the foundation of an effective leadership training program.

The first is *motivation*. Motivation is essential to the effective function of any organization. If an organization has proper goals, leadership must be motivated toward them. James Kouzes and Barry Posner in *The Leadership*

Challenge, remind us that challenge is a major factor in motivation.

> If leaders wish to get the best from others, they must search for opportunities for people to create or outdo themselves. Leaders must find opportunities for people to solve problems, make discoveries, explore new ground, reach a difficult goal, or figure out how to deal with an external threat. And they must make it fun.[28]

To put it another way, we need to take a "human resources view" of leadership training. The new leader must not only be taught how to put round pegs in round holes but must also be encouraged to develop a total view of how he or she fits into the work of the entire organization.

The second ingredient is the matter of job description or *performance standards*. New leaders should have a written role definition explaining precisely what is expected of them in the organization and what they may expect of their superiors. Too often people complain, "I'm not sure that's my responsibility," or, "I never know how I'm doing at my job." Both attitudes lead to insecurity and frustration; you want to build the opposite attitudes as early as possible.

A third crucial factor is the *delineation of organizational objectives*. These were discussed in an earlier chapter with an emphasis on both the total objectives of the organization and the importance of fitting personal goals into them. What *you* have learned, you now teach to your leadership trainee. As the leaders identify with ministry objectives, they learn to fit their own life-style and meaningful life goals into the total perspective.

A trusting and respecting relationship toward all workers is an essential ingredient to success in ministry. You want the new leader to be a part of that kind of climate and to foster the spirit of cooperation you have been trying to build.

Evaluating performance

When you agree to take a leadership post, you agree to evaluate the work of your subordinates and to give them some kind of "grade" on their levels of performance. You particularly evaluate those new leaders who are brought into the organization as a part of your recruitment plan. Much of your review and appraisal of coworkers will be subjective; that is, you will be forming judgments on the basis of what you see and hear about them rather than on a formal rating form.

The relationship of evaluation to job description and objectives is so crucial that to ignore it invites disaster in the entire evaluation process. If your new leaders know exactly what is expected of them, then you can determine whether or not they are producing those results. If, however, they are confused as to what is expected of them, then your evaluation-and-performance interview with them will only create further confusion and frustration for both of you. Be sure to give reasons for every judgment you make. This will help you eliminate personal prejudice and prepare a more valuable analysis.

Sometimes you will want to use self-evaluation to measure how well a trainee thinks he or she has accomplished the goals and objectives of the position. This usually leads to a personal interview between supervisor and worker, and you can learn a great deal about your new leader's problems and strengths at this point. You then become a counselor and guide in helping the person to change some methodology or to approach his or her task differently.

Organizations must discriminate between success and failure by setting standards related to institutional goals. Here are some guidelines to use when setting up those all-important standards.

1. Be sure your standards are as specific and as objective as they can be. Relate them to biblical imperatives whenever possible.
2. Be sure that both you and your new leader agree upon the importance of these standards before he or she begins work.
3. Do not be afraid to revise the standards if a change in the work conditions warrants such revision.
4. Always evaluate the leader's performance in relation to these standards.
5. Be careful of time deadlines. It takes some people more time to work up to a satisfactory performance level, but often when they reach that level, they maintain a better consistency than the "rapid-rise," but fluctuating, type of leader.
6. Do not develop unrealistic or idealistic standards that cannot be met.

Both Christ and Paul followed these principles in their work with disciples and early leaders in the church. Our Lord had only three and one-half years to train a small group of men upon whose shoulders rested the entire cause of Christianity. His methods were clearly person-centered, and He successfully committed His leadership to His followers so that they went out to turn their world upside down. His pattern of personally developing a small group has never been improved upon in the history of leadership science.

Evaluation of a leader's performance is a difficult aspect of your responsibility, but it is a necessary one. Willard

Claassen suggests five questions you might ask after you have observed the new recruit in association with his or her work group:

1. Was leadership distributed among group members?
2. Were there "status struggles" in the group? In other words, were several or more members in the group struggling for leadership?
3. Was there a power structure or hidden agenda?
4. Was the leader autocratic? paternalistic? or democratic?
5. What kind of control did the leader exert (as seen in ease of movement, treatment of absentees or latecomers)? What were the attitudes of the group toward leadership?[29]

Did our Lord use a distinctive pattern in recruiting workers? Certainly His methods were not static. He knew the secret of dealing with every person as an individual. Certain central ideas do emerge, however. For example, He always spent much time in prayer relative to the selection of leaders. He always provided careful training for their task and challenged them with the importance of that task in the light of God's authority. Furthermore, He selected workers who fit predetermined standards. That is, He did not try to recruit just anybody for leadership. With the exception of Judas, the disciples, as different as they were in their individual personalities, did display some common characteristics:

1. They were unspoiled by religious tradition.
2. They were open-minded and hungry for the truth.
3. They were willing to follow their leader.
4. They possessed loyalty and enthusiasm for their work.

5. They were willing to make sacrifices.
6. They served from a pure motive.

The 10th chapter of the Gospel of Luke records the sending and return of the 70 workers recruited by the Lord. They came back with joy because they had experienced positive opportunities in service. That experience was not accidental. It was the clear result of proper enlistment patterns exemplified in our Lord's ministry.

NOTES

1. Andrew W. Halpin. *Theory and Research in Administration*. New York: Macmillian Publishing Co., Inc., 1966, p. 83. Reprinted by permission.

2. J.W. Alexander. *Managing Our Work*. Downers Grove, IL: Inter-Varsity Press, 1972.

3. Kenneth O. Gangel. *Building Leaders for Church Education*. Chicago, IL: Moody Press, 1981, ch. 11 and *Feeding and Leading*. Wheaton, IL: Victor Books, 1989, ch. 4.

4. Charles H. Ford. "Are You Geared to Problems or Objectives?" *TWA Ambassador*, (March/April 1970), p. 27. Used by permission.

5. Four steps in italics, Ford, p. 29.

6. Ford, p. 29.

7. Louis A. Allen. *The Management Profession*. New York: McGraw-Hill Book Company, 1964, p. 97. Used by permission.

8. Allen, p. 97.

9. J.D. Batten. *Tough-minded Management*. New York: American Management Association, 1963, pp. 55–56. Used by permission.

10. Ken Blanchard. "The Extremes of Leadership," *Church Management—The Clergy Journal*, (Nov. Dec. 1986), p. 8.

11. *The Philosophical Works of Descartes, I*, tr. by Elizabeth S. Haldane and G.R.T. Ross. London: Cambridge University Press, 1911, pp. 92–92.

12. Howard K. Holland. "Decision Making and Personality," *Personnel Administration*, May-June 1968, pp. 24–29.

13. Edward de Bono. "The Virtues of Zigzag Thinking," *Think*, Vol. 35, No. 3, (May–June 1969), pp. 7–11. Used by permission.

14. de Bono, p. 9.

15. Kimball Wiles. "The Communications Explosion," *The Teacher's Guide to the 21st Century.* Syracuse, NY: Educational Press Association of America. Used by permission.

16. William V. Haney. "How to Say What You Mean," *Nation's Business*—the Chamber of Commerce the United States. Reprinted from May issue by permission.

17. Edgar Dale. "Good Reasons for Doing Nothing," *The News Letter* (December 1960), Bureau of Educational Research and Service, Ohio State University. Used by permission.

18. Charles E. Hancock. "When and How to Use Small Groups." From *Church Administration*, The Sunday School Board of the Southern Baptists Convention, 1971. All rights reserved. Used by permission.

19. Hancock, p. 30.

20. Reuel Howe. "Training for a Time of Change," *The Christian Century* (April 22, 1970). Reprinted by permission.

21. Grant Howard, unpublished class notes, Dallas Theological Seminary.

22. General Henry M. Robert. *Robert's Rules of Order*, Glenview, IL: Scott, Foresman and Company, 1970.

23. Gangel, p. 137. Used by permission.

24. Sidney Sutherland. *When You Preside.* Danville, IL: The Interstate Printers and Publishers, Inc., 1952. Used by permission.

25. Quoted in Chambers Williams "Macho-Management: It Has No Place in Today's Business." *Phoenix Business Journal* (July 7, 1986), p. 4.

26. Roy B. Zuck. "The Superintendent and Teacher Enlistment," Wheaton, IL: Scripture Press Ministries Superintendent's Monograph. Used by permission.

27. Ted Engstrom and Edward Dayton. "Hiring," *Christian Leadership Letter* (June 1987), p. 2.

28. James M. Kouzes and Barry Z. Posner. *The Leadership Challenge*. San Francisco: Josey-Bass, 1987. pp. 46–47.

29. Willard Claasen. *Learning to Lead*. Scottsdale, PA: Herald Press and Newton, KS: Faith and Life Press, 1963. Used by permission.